MURDERING THE PRESIDENT

MURDERING THE
PRESIDENT

ALEXANDER GRAHAM BELL
AND THE RACE TO SAVE
JAMES GARFIELD

FRED ROSEN | FOREWORD BY HANK GARFIELD

POTOMAC BOOKS
AN IMPRINT OF THE UNIVERSITY OF NEBRASKA PRESS

∞

Library of Congress Cataloging-in-Publication Data
Names: Rosen, Fred, author.
Title: Murdering the president: Alexander Graham Bell and
the race to save James Garfield / Fred Rosen; foreword by
Hank Garfield.
Description: Lincoln: Potomac Books, an imprint of the
University of Nebraska Press, 2016. | Includes bibliographical
references and index.
Identifiers: LCCN 2016003751
ISBN 9781612347684 (cloth: alk. paper)
ISBN 9781612348636 (epub)
ISBN 9781612348643 (mobi)
ISBN 9781612348650 (pdf)
Subjects: LCSH: Garfield, James A. (James Abram),
1831–1881—Death and burial. | Garfield, James A. (James
Abram), 1831–1881—Assassination. | Bell, Alexander Graham,
1847–1922. | Bliss, Willard, 1825–1889.
Classification: LCC E687.9 .R67 2016 | DDC 973.8/4092—dc23
LC record available at http://lccn.loc.gov/2016003751

Set in Lyon Text by Rachel Gould.

For my father, PFC Murray Rosen, U.S. Army,
who served his adopted country with
valor during World War II, and though he died in 1983,
before any of my books were published,
bequeathed to me his love of American history

CONTENTS

ILLUSTRATIONS

FOREWORD

Hank Garfield

Fred Rosen first called me in the fall of 2004, a few months after the publication of my young-adult historical novel, *The Lost Voyage of John Cabot.*

The book's jacket flap and some blurbs on the Internet had identified me as the great-great-grandson of President James A. Garfield. That fact had also been on the jacket of my first novel, *Moondog*, a werewolf whodunit set in the hills of California, and published ten years earlier. Fred explained that he wrote true crime books, with an emphasis on investigative reporting.

Most of his work covered modern cases. Now Fred was interested in the historical drama surrounding my great-great-grandfather's death. We talked for a while, about the writing business, my famous ancestor, and Fred's belief as to what the real story was: Alexander Graham Bell raced to save my great-great-grandfather, while Dr. Willard Bliss deliberately did the direct opposite.

"You're not what I expected," Fred said, after we had spoken for awhile.

"How so?" I asked him.

"Well, you sound like a pretty normal guy. I thought I was going to get one of the Kennedys on the phone."

I was sitting at my computer in my bathrobe, playing spider solitaire, and sucking down the day's first cup of coffee. How much more normal can you get?

I live in Maine. I make a modest living as a college English teacher and magazine writer. I've published five novels. I've raised two kids, mostly by myself, and I don't own a car. I drink beer and follow the Red Sox. I *am* a pretty normal guy.

James Abram Garfield left a lot of descendants. The president had four sons who lived to adulthood, and they all had sons, and most of their sons had sons, and those family cells scattered, as Americans do, all across the country.

Add in the different-named descendants of daughters on various branches of the family tree, and we could stage a good-sized reunion at the White House. We could do it on the president's birthday, November 19, or on the date he was shot in the Washington train station, July 2. Or, we could all gather on the Jersey Shore to commemorate the day he died, September 19.

Garfield's presidency may have been a blip on the radar screen of American history, but he left an extensive living legacy, which is more than George Washington did. We're not a close-knit clan. At my grandfather Garfield's funeral in Concord, Massachusetts, in 1979, I met relatives I'd never known I had. Fewer people made it to Maine in the summer of 2006 to say good-bye to my father, killed in a car accident in North Carolina.

Cousins of cousins, all related to that long-dead president. It was never a big deal to me. When you're a kid, it takes a while to realize who you are, and that there's such a thing as a class structure, and that you are peering out at the world from one of its shelves. But James Garfield's upbringing had more in common with Bill Clinton's than John Kennedy's.

He was the smartest kid in his one-room rural school, and he worked his way up to become a schoolteacher, a general in the Civil War, and a member of the U.S. Congress. His son Harry became president of the president's alma mater, Williams College. Harry's son—my grandfather—became a medical doctor and married into a family that owned property on the coast of Maine.

My father, a high-school math teacher, enjoyed a comfortable retirement from the sale of that property, right up until his sudden death at the age of eighty in March 2006. My family did have enough money to send me to St. Paul's School, an elite prep school in New Hampshire. At St. Paul's the presidential pedigree wasn't special.

The school was filled with the sons and daughters of influential families. My own family history was in evidence on the crew plaques that lined the corridors of the gym. All four of the president's sons attended St. Paul's in the 1880s and 1890s, and all were apparently good rowers.

One of my classmates at St. Paul's was Senator Robert Kennedy's son Michael, who would meet his own tragic death on a ski slope before his fortieth birthday. We knew each other, but weren't friends. Sometimes we found ourselves in the same group, though, and I recall one conversation around a backgammon game about the Garfield chin and the Kennedy nose.

I wish I'd had the presence of mind during our time together at St. Paul's to ask Michael what it was like to lose a father to political assassination. He would have been ten or eleven years old at the time. It must have been devastating. I never saw him again after St. Paul's. By the time he died, I was living in California, clinging to the edge of the continent by means of a couple of journalism jobs and a just-published first novel.

A murder can reverberate through a family for generations, but the assassination of President Garfield was ancient history as far as I was concerned. I seldom thought about it, and I don't remember it being discussed around the family dinner table. Most of what I knew about the president's life and death came not from family sources but from books, read long after high school.

When speculation swirled in the press in 1988 that the Democrats could be headed for a brokered convention, I researched and wrote a piece for the *San Diego Union* about the Republican convention of 1880, which had nominated Garfield, a compromise candidate in a deadlock between Ulysses S. Grant and James G. Blaine, on the thirty-sixth ballot.

On a cross-country trip, I took the kids to the Garfield homestead and museum in Mentor, Ohio, outside of Cleveland, where we saw an upholstered chair, specially constructed with one side higher than the other to enable Garfield to pour his six-foot-plus frame across it and assume a comfortable position for reading at night.

I learned that Garfield was the first president to use a telephone in the White House, and that Alexander Graham Bell had attempted to save the president's life following the shooting, by employing a prototype of a metal detector to locate the bullet that had lodged near his spine. I also learned that he was one of the few true scholars to occupy the White House.

One legend holds that he could write Latin with one hand and Greek with the other. He is credited with an original proof of the Pythagorean theorem, using the formula for the area of a trapezoid. He was known by his contemporaries as a complex man and deep thinker who could see all sides of an issue, a trait his political opponents derided as weakness.

Had he lived, I believe America would have seen his backbone. I base this opinion not only on written history but also on the well-observed Garfield trait, shared by most of my relatives, of flexibility up to a certain point and firm resolve thereafter.

The president stood up to Roscoe Conkling, a powerful senator of his own party, over political appointments in Conkling's home state of New York. Conkling had backed Ulysses Grant for a third term at the contentious Republican convention.

Garfield moved to investigate and remedy corruption in the U.S. Postal Service, by seeking to end the bribery and awarding of postal delivery contracts via the "star route" system that served the rural West. At the four-month mark of his presidency, my great-great-grandfather was just getting his feet under him. He was poised to become the capable leader his admirers knew he could be.

To me, that's the lasting tragedy of the Garfield presidency— what could have been.

Imagine if John F. Kennedy had been gunned down *before* the Cuban Missile Crisis, before Alan Shepard's suborbital flight, and the bold declaration that we would put a man on the moon by the end of the decade. How would history remember him? James Garfield was just forty-nine when he died.

Too young, too young. Too much left undone.

PREFACE

This story began at the William L. Clements Library of the University of Michigan at Ann Arbor. There I discovered an original copy of the 1883 *American Journal of Science*. It contained Alexander Graham Bell's long-forgotten paper on the attempted assassination of President James Garfield and the great American inventor's heroic efforts to create twentieth-century technology in the nineteenth century to save the president's life.

That was the beginning. It then took me fourteen years to finally unravel this murder case. I was lucky it took me that long. This book includes recently discovered medical reports relating to new details of the care President Garfield actually received from his chief physician, Dr. Doctor Willard Bliss. Supporting a forensic examination of the historical record, those reports reflect directly on who is really responsible for James Garfield's murder.

The Rainbow City

Buffalo, September 6, 1901

Robert Todd Lincoln was late. Maybe it was because he had such short, stumpy legs. Or at least that's what his father thought.

When Robert was only three years old, Abraham Lincoln wrote, "Bob is short and low and, I expect, always will be."[1]

Boy, that's pressure.

"Honest Abe" was not taking into consideration his own immense six-foot-four height, which influenced his perspective heavily. To him, Robert, at five foot nine, was "sawed off." He was also his oldest surviving son. Maybe that was why he was so hard on him. Whatever it was, Robert knew his father would have chastised him for his perpetual lateness.

Robert was fifty-eight years old and as successful as a man could get. He had already served two presidents as secretary of war and one as minister to Great Britain. Robert led a successful Chicago law firm, which in turn led to him becoming the president of the Pullman Company. Yet that tall shadow of his father's, in the stovepipe hat with that benevolent expression, was forever stalking him. He later wrote,

> During my childhood and early youth he was almost constantly away from home, attending courts or making political speeches. In 1859 when I was sixteen, and when he was beginning to devote himself more to practice in his own neighborhood, and when I would have both the inclination and the means of gratifying my desire to become better acquainted with the history of his struggles, I went to New Hampshire to school and afterward to Harvard College, and he became President.

Henceforth, any great intimacy between us became impossible. I scarcely even had ten minutes quiet talk with him during his Presidency, on account of his constant devotion to business.

Perhaps Robert's close friend, Nicholas Murray Butler, provided the answer, when he wrote that Robert revered his father's memory so much that he lived under its shadow. According to Butler, Robert often said that he was *not* Robert Lincoln but Abraham Lincoln's son: "No one wanted me for Secretary of War, they wanted *Abraham Lincoln's son*. No one wanted me for minister to England; they wanted *Abraham Lincoln's son*. No one wanted me for president of the Pullman Company; they wanted *Abraham Lincoln's son*."[2]

Robert stumped faster.

Hours earlier, Robert's train had arrived at Buffalo's Central Station from Chicago. As president of the company that actually invented the sleeping car, Robert's had been nicely outfitted, befitting his station.

Where the 1893 World's Columbian Exposition in Chicago had been nicknamed "the White City," because all the buildings were painted white, Buffalo's 1903 Pan-American Exposition used boldly applied colors on buildings and statuary to make the place look like a multicolored fairy palace when it was lit up at night—"the Rainbow City."

Walking still faster through the Rainbow City, Robert could hear the water spewing from the Electric Fountains. When President William McKinley called and asked if he would meet him at the Pan-American Exposition, Robert of course had said yes.

From scanning the Buffalo morning papers on the trolley that took him from the train station to the exposition's gate, Robert knew that the president's speech the day before had gone well. Today, he was just going to shake hands. President McKinley figured he'd have some time afterward to chat with Robert about some disturbing dreams he'd been having lately.

As he rounded the corner, the sound of the fountains was

absorbed by the shouts of twenty thousand people clamoring for a chance to shake the president's hand. They surrounded the Temple of Music, a bizarre-looking building that looked like a cake left out too long in the sun. The melted part was really the outer perimeter, a square of red curlicues trimmed in gold and yellow, topped by statuary of famous composers. In the center, the cake's top, was a vast dome with a red field and blue-green detailing.[3]

It was a hot, humid day, and at a little before 4:00 p.m., President McKinley was already in the receiving line in the pavilion when Robert got there. Unlike most of the exposition's buildings, the interior of the Temple of Music was finished, the walls red with green bronze panels and ivory curlicues. Robert was afraid he was too late for his appointment with one of his father's successors.

Inside the pavilion, there was a long line of about two hundred people waiting in the queue to shake McKinley's hand. The secret service agents guarding the president spotted Leon Czolgosz very quickly. How could they not, with that mop of flaming red hair and his right hand thrust beneath the lapel of his coat?

A handkerchief was wrapped around it, giving the impression that the hand or one of its digits was injured. He was conservatively dressed. His smooth-shaven cheeks made him seem like a young man barely into his twenties. Czolgosz extended his left hand to the president. Suspecting nothing, McKinley put out his right hand to shake Czolgosz's.

Czolgosz shot out his left hand and grabbed the president's forearm in a viselike grip, pulling him slightly forward, while at the same time, his right hand came out from the coat holding a pistol that he pressed into McKinley's chest.[4]

Robert was about to move through the crowd to introduce himself, when he heard the two shots ring out. He didn't run; Robert knew it was too late for that. He'd been on General Grant's staff in 1865; he knew gunfire. Instead, Robert stopped and stood stock-still, rooted to the spot.

Watching, feeling as the crowd surged around him, Robert's thoughts raced back two decades, to the Baltimore and Potomac Railroad Station on the Washington Mall. On July 2, 1881, President James Garfield had gone there to board a southbound train. He was going to see his wife, Lucretia, in New Jersey. Serving the president as his secretary of war, Robert had accompanied him to the train station.

Charles Guiteau attempted to assassinate President Garfield. But the president had not succumbed to the bullet. With the president moved over to the White House for care of his bullet wound, Robert Lincoln took over. He immediately summoned Dr. D. Willard Bliss to oversee the president's care.

Bliss was James Garfield's oldest friend. Sort of.

MURDERING THE PRESIDENT

ONE

When the first slaver put
out for the Congo,
I stood on her deck.

—Stephen Vincent Benét,
"The Devil and Daniel
Webster"

"Circumstances Have Led Me into Both Callings"

Ohio, 1851

He could not afford a horse, he could not afford train fare, he could not afford *anything*. Instead, twenty-year-old James Abram Garfield did the only thing he could do under the circumstances—he struck out by foot, southeast, down a dusty road, leading toward the Western Eclectic Institute in Hiram, Ohio.[1]

All of his subsequent biographers would point out that James Garfield was the last of his breed—a future president born in a log cabin, as if this was something noble. Who lived in a cabin on the Ohio frontier? Poor settlers, who could afford nothing better in the nearby slums of Cleveland on Lake Erie, fourteen miles away. When he decided to go to college, Garfield left behind him the most brutal of poverty.

That log cabin his biographers glorified was a built by his father, Abram, and quickly, in January 1830, in northern Ohio, less than twenty miles from Lake Erie. It was either that or perish in the cold of winter. Abram sealed the cracks in the logs with mud and wood chips. He was a good carpenter, but despite his best efforts, the building materials at his disposal produced a sad, gray, drafty affair.

The inside walls of the cabin still had spaces where the muddy wood chips hadn't hardened properly. His wife, Eliza, used cloth and clay to fill them up. As for the floor, it was good old mother earth. It would have to do. Young James was born the following year on November 19, 1831. Less than eighteen months later, Abram left the cabin one early evening.

He came home late, his clothes covered in soot. Abram had

been helping his neighbors fight a forest fire that was threatening their homes. Coughing violently, he had inhaled too much smoke and exerted himself to exhaustion. He soon got the chills. Fluid filled his lungs. Eliza tried to help her husband, but he was dying of pneumonia. There was no cure.

"Eliza, you will soon be alone," he whispered to her on his deathbed. "We have planted four saplings in these woods. I leave them to your care."

Abram died in Eliza's arms, leaving her to care for their four children, alone. All they had was a farm in a forest in northern Ohio that Abram had barely begun to clear. It took years for even the stoutest of men to cut his place from the forest and make it his own; and yet Eliza Garfield, née Ballou, decided to do it on her own, and with the help she fervently believed would be provided by Divine Providence.

Besides sweet baby James, Abram had left Eliza with three other children: Thomas, ten years old; and sisters Mary, nine years old, and Hetty, seven years old. Being the oldest, Thomas shouldered the family burden as soon as he was able. He foreswore an education to work hard on the farm, so his little brother and sisters could have a chance at a better life.

James Garfield grew up to be a little over six feet tall and a rawhide, muscular two hundred pounds. He had a talent for repairing and making things with his hands. Like his father, he was good with tools. Awkward and self-educated, he loved reading adventure novels, which gave him sailing aspirations.[2]

Garfield had struck out from home once before, at sixteen, to work on a canal boat that plied the narrow waters between Cleveland and Pittsburgh. In only six weeks as a canal-boat driver, he made himself a reputation for efficiently piloting a small boat pulled by mules through a small body of water. He also got into a fight with a fellow driver, eighteen years his senior. With the crew watching, young Garfield found himself dodging a wildly thrown but powerful right hand.

Garfield countered with a powerful left behind the miscreant's left ear that sent him to his knees and ended the fight.

"Hurrah for Mr. Garfield!" shouted the crew, including Harry Brown, a sailor from south of the Mason Dixon Line.

Soon after his big "win," Garfield fell violently ill. He was diagnosed with ague. He didn't know it, but he had been bitten by an infected mosquito that had then given him malaria, as the disease would be known later. Returning home to convalesce, he had what can only be described as an epiphany. If he stayed on the road he was then on, he would die an unhappy manual laborer. Something inside told him he was better than that.

Dr. J. P. Robison was a physician in nearby Bedford. He was known to be a good judge of men. Garfield presented himself to the doctor in his front parlor.

"My name is James Garfield. My home is at Orange. I have acquired only the rudiments of an education, and but a scanty knowledge of books. But, at this time, I have taken up the notion of getting an education, and, before beginning, I want to know what I have to count on. You are a physician, and know men well. Examine me, and say plainly whether you think I will be able to succeed."

The doctor appreciated the young man's candor. He gave him the courtesy of a complete examination and then pronounced judgment.

"You are well fitted to follow your profession, as far as you please to go."

He eyed Garfield's large head and then his body.

"Your brain is large and good; your physique is adapted to hard work. Go ahead and you are sure to succeed."

With the doctor's sage advice sounding in his ears, Garfield footed it up the road to the Western Eclectic Institute in Hiram. He had just fifteen dollars: a ten-dollar bill in an old leather pocketbook, which was in the breast pocket of his coat, and the other five in his trousers' pocket.

As the day was hot, he took his coat off. Carrying it on his arm, he took good care to feel every moment or two for the pocketbook. The hard-earned fifteen dollars was to pay his entrance at the college. As his journey progressed, Garfield got to thinking about what college life would be like, and forgot all about the pocketbook. When he went to look for it, it was gone.

He went back, searching frantically along the road, hunting on both sides for the pocketbook. After awhile, he came to a house where a young man was casually leaning over a gate.

"What are you hunting for?" the young man questioned.

"A wallet has fallen out of my jacket pocket," Garfield explained.

As if by a conjurer's magic, the young man handed him the wallet.

"You saved me for college," said Garfield, barely containing the emotion in his voice. "I will not forget that. What is your name?"

"D. Willard Bliss," the young man smiled and extended his hand.

Garfield extended his. "James Garfield."

In the moment that they shook hands, a lifelong friendship was forged. These two men would be linked in ways they never could have imagined. As D. Willard, who was known to his family as "D. W.," watched James Garfield walk back down the road, he went back to his packing. He was already a twenty-five-year-old medical doctor with a special interest in surgery.

In his doctor's bag, he made sure to pack in his scalpel set and Nelaton probe. He turned his horse-drawn wagon onto the same road James Garfield had taken, but in the opposite direction.

His given name was actually "Doctor," after a "Doctor Willard" of Auburn, New York, who had delivered him. But as he grew up, he became known as D. W. Especially considering his later profession, it might have been confusing to call him "Doctor Doctor." Bliss's parents, Obediah and Marilla, came from Massachusetts, but eventually settled in New York.

Bliss was born in 1825. As soon as he was born, the family packed up, like many Americans had been doing for generations, this time traversing the Alleghenies. They settled in Ohio. By the time James Garfield met him that day in 1851, the twenty-five-year-old Bliss had already graduated from Western Reserve

College as a physician, married Ohio-born Sophia Prentiss, and had their first child, Ellis Baker.

The road the Bliss family took that day from their Ohio home, eventually led to Grand Rapids, Michigan. One of the first things Bliss felt when they arrived was the cool breeze coming off Lake Superior, ten miles to the west. It was a verdant green wonderland in summer. But the winters were brutal, temperatures plummeting below zero on a regular basis.

Bliss moved his family into the third floor of Miller's Boarding House on Ledyard Street and expeditiously set up his medical practice. Grand Rapids was a bustling town. Bliss located his office on Nevius Street, between Pearl and Justice Avenues. Seeking as much business as he could get, his shingle read, "Surgeon, Oculist and Aurist."

The former was an eye specialist, the latter an ear specialist. Bliss was neither. But he needed to make a living. Besides, there was no law against advertising yourself as a medical specialist in areas you weren't proficient in. There was nothing illegal about that. Ethics was another matter.

Coming from a musically gifted family, Bliss was a bon vivant who enjoyed sitting at the piano and pounding out tunes. While people sang around him, his own tenor's voice was the strongest and loudest. Yet despite his immersion in the arts, nothing could take him away from his work as a surgeon. Since Grand Rapids was a logging community, accidents involving extremities were all too common. Much of his practice involved amputations.

Rather than allow gangrene to set in, arms, legs, and fingers damaged in one accident or another were usually amputated. Even if the patient survived the amputation, there was a good chance blood poisoning would occur. Often organ failure and death followed.

Noticing early in his career the value of good publicity, Bliss allowed a reporter from the *Enquirer*, a local paper, to observe an amputation, in which a colleague assisted him. The story was reported in the paper on January 5, 1856:

The poor fellow was well known about town under the appellation of Jelka, and until the last year or two, was in the employ of A. D. Rathbone, Esq. Nearly a year ago, he was kicked on the left leg by a horse, since which time the limb has continually grown worse, until at last it became necessary to amputate it, in order to save his life.

Doctors D. W. and Henderson performed the operation in capital style, Dr. B., wielding the knife, and taking it off above the knee. The patient being under the influence of chloroform, was not aware until told, that the major part of his limb was detached from his body. It was a painful sight to witness. We never saw chloroform administered before in a surgical operation, and we never wish to see another, unless it is administered. It is truly the sufferer's solace, and a blessed painkiller.

This would not be the last time Bliss used the press to promote himself.[3]

• • •

A few years later, James Garfield made Dr. J. P. Robison extremely proud when he not only graduated from Western Eclectic but took off for Williams College in Massachusetts for a graduate degree. But before he left, he had started to teach classes in Greek. Lucretia Rudolph, a teenager who, like Garfield, worshiped as a Disciple of Christ, was one of his students. He didn't forget her. Smart and attractive, her daddy had helped found Western Eclectic.

It was while attending Williams that Garfield began to pay close attention to the political debate about slavery.

"This subject is entirely new to me. I am going to know all about it," he told a friend.

In Massachusetts, the westerner was being asked to decide on the issue of the day—should the slaves be freed or continue to remain enslaved to subsidize the economy of the southern United States?

He voraciously tore into everything he could get his hands

"CIRCUMSTANCES HAVE LED ME"

on about slavery—pamphlets, broadsheets, scientific journals, magazines, and books. After a profound and careful study of the history of slavery and the heroic resistance to it, Garfield came to see slavery as clearly wrong. It was his mother, after all, who had made him study the Bible and helped hone his skills as a local preacher.

At the Williams College campus, he used his religious speaking experience and attracted crowds where he openly condemned the institution of slavery and demanded its demise. Upon graduation, his fellow students voted him most likely to be a member of Congress in ten years. They were off by just a few.

While attending Williams, Garfield sent a note to Lucretia Rudolph. Like him, she taught at Western Eclectic after graduating. She taught French, algebra, and Latin. Then, proud to be "on her own," she moved to Ravenna, Ohio, to take a teaching job. After receiving James's note, they began a long correspondence. But James had a problem with Lucretia, whom he began to call "Crete."

"I have a fear of commitment to someone who does not display outright emotion or give freely of physical affection," he wrote her.

When Crete came to attend his graduation from Williams College, she was naturally disturbed when James introduced her to another young woman, Rebecca Selleck. James admitted to her that he and Rebecca had had a romance. It couldn't have lasted long. Western Eclectic offered James a position as an instructor in ancient languages.

Garfield went back to Ohio and so did Crete. But not before they reached an understanding that they would get married in the future. Crete left her teaching job in Ravenna, all set to be a wife. But when that didn't happen as quickly as she would have liked, Crete took a new job teaching in Cleveland.[4]

Back at Western Eclectic, Garfield was making quite a name for himself.

"He took very kindly to me, and assisted me in various ways because I was poor and was janitor of the buildings and swept them out in the morning and built the fires, as he had done only six years before, when he was a pupil at the same school," said J. L. Darsie, a student of Garfield's.

"He was a tall, strong man, full of animal spirits, but dreadfully awkward," Darsie observed. "He used to run out on the green almost every day and play cricket with us. Every now and then he would get a hit on the nose and he muffed his ball and lost his hat as a regular thing. He was left handed too, and that made him seem all the clumsier."

"But he was most powerful and very quick and it was easy for us to understand how it was that he had acquired the reputation of whipping all the other mule-drivers on the [Pennsylvania] canal, and of making himself the hero of that thoroughfare when he followed its tow path ten years earlier."

Garfield became so popular and respected that at twenty-six, he became the school's youngest college president, ever. That, however, was not enough for his mother, Eliza. She wanted more. His mother had become the most powerful influence in his life after his father died. At his mother's behest, Garfield had become an accomplished preacher at prayer gatherings.

Yet neither profession, teaching or preaching, gave him the true emotional and spiritual satisfaction he coveted.

"Circumstances have led me into both callings," he told a friend. "The desire of brethren to have me preach and teach for them, a desire to do good in all ways that I could, and in noble callings to earn something to pay my way through a course of study, and to discharge debts, have led me to both callings. [But] I have never intended to devote my life to either or both."[5]

And then Garfield received the piece of luck that would catapult him into a profession that, in some ways, combined both preaching and teaching.

2

"First Fruit"

Edinburgh, Scotland

To his family and friends, Alexander Bell was known as "Alec."[1] Unlike his two brothers and his father, he had been christened without a middle name. As he was growing up, that really bothered him.

Alec was born March 3, 1847, in an insignificant flat off Charlotte Square, a centuries-old series of large, Georgian structures next to a beautiful park in the middle of Edinburgh. Next to London, it was the second-most powerful city in the British Empire. The city's power came, literally, from the mind.

Edinburgh's men of letters came forth with powerful intellectual and scientific thought, advancing humanity through practical knowledge and invention. Alexander Melville Bell, who friends and family referred to as Melville, was an innovative speech teacher, who taught and wrote about the subject extensively. He was Alec's father.

A few years after Alec's birth, Melville Bell had achieved enough success financially that he was able to move his wife, Eliza, and their three boys to a suite of ten rooms on two floors, right across the square from their old home, but this time with a view of the park. The Bell family had finally arrived!

It was an accident of birth that Alexander Bell and James Garfield, the two men who would later make history together, had mothers with the same first name. In Eliza Symonds's case, she had been born partially deaf. Eliza could speak, however— the result of an outstanding intellect, a voracious appetite for knowledge, and a refusal to give up or give in. That stubbornness was a trait she would later pass on to Alec.

When Eliza's brothers, with whom she was close, left home to conquer the world, she had refused to succumb to loneliness. She read and soon began to paint. She realized she had an aptitude as a painter of miniatures. By the time she was thirty-five, she was well accomplished and living with her widowed mother. Eliza was a spinster, with a decent dowry. Then Alexander Melville Bell came along.

Melville certainly cared about what money could buy. But he would not compromise his principles for it. Nor his heart. He was a speech and elocution teacher, and as good with his voice as Abram Garfield had been with his hammer. At a time when men tended to marry women younger than themselves, Melville Bell was a decade younger than Eliza. They met through mutual friends.

"I have apartments you can rent," Eliza soon told Melville.

There was a flat he could rent that was part of her home. A smitten Melville was only too happy to oblige. A perfect gentleman, he insisted upon calling at the front door to take Eliza out. Melville was a smart, attractive young man who had not wanted for female companionship. But Eliza was different.

Despite her hearing difficulties, she hadn't allowed the silence she lived with most of her life to isolate her. Her miniatures reached out to the world; they were much sought after by collectors. Melville was a great admirer of art and had his own collection of miniatures. There was much they had in common. Melville fell madly in love, as did Eliza.

Engaged six months later, they soon married. Eliza Bell was a woman of churchly rectitude. When Alec was born, she took him with her to church, every Sunday. But even Christ's companionship was not enough for the youngster. As he grew, Alec kept pleading with his father to give him a middle name.

In the downstairs part of their home, there was a small flat for a boarder. Melville rented it to Alexander Graham, one of his students. Alec loved the name "Graham," and he decided to take it for his long-overdue middle name. Alec announced to his family that he would be known as A. Graham Bell. On March 3, 1858, on Alec's eleventh birthday, it became official.

Melville gave an eloquent toast to honor his son's choice of a middle name. All the family joined in on congratulating Alec. A middle name was as unique a birthday present as anyone ever got. And he had taken it himself. But it made no difference what his name was—Alec's mind wandered. He could never satisfy his imagination.

His brain raced at the speed of light. He kept getting ideas. And while Alec's intellect was growing, so was his father Melville's. Phonetics was Melville Bell's particular interest. His business had expanded, as he established his unique system of Visible Speech to communicate with the deaf. And as his reputation grew, so did his business.

Between the money he made from teaching, elocution lessons, and publishing, Melville Bell was able to purchase a country cottage, which the family visited a few times a month, weather, of course, permitting. It was there, at the country cottage, that Alec and neighbor Ben Herdman became friends.

They'd run off to play in britches and work shirts, their boots crunching on the dead leaves and sinking in the muck of the riverbank. Ben's sister Annie would later remember looking at Alec Bell in his teen years and thinking, "How tall and handsome he was, with long black hair, which he had a trick of always throwing it back."[2]

When they discovered the mill, run by John Herdman, Ben's father, it was a place of wonder and excitement to the two twelve-year-olds. They saw strange pieces of wood and metal made into odd shapes that were scattered around on the yellow, wheat-dust-encrusted floor. These were the bones of old pieces of farm machinery, scavenged from dying mills.

And then there were the usual implements of the farmer's trade—hoes, rakes, water buckets, harnesses, and knives. Throughout the place were piles of wheat, waiting to be husked. As a young child, Alec had gotten lost in a wheat field. It was his earliest memory. He learned how dense it was and what it meant to be alone.

John Herdman had seen the boys rummaging through the mills, their excited voices discussing their "finds." Getting tired of the boys expending energy on unproductive activities, he invited them to his office, and Herdman got right to the point.

"Now boys, why don't you do something useful?"

"What needs to be done at the mill?" Alec asked pointedly.

Herdman opened a sack of unhusked wheat at his feet.

"If only you could take the husks off this wheat, you would be doing something useful indeed."

Herdman watched as the boy went back onto the mill floor. Alec's mind was racing. He of all people knew what would be needed to demystify the wheat. Then he acted, racing around the barn, searching for specific things. He began taking common items from around the mill, including some nails and especially the brushes.

Yes, the brushes!

Taking his haul to a worktable, Alec set it down. The idea was to create a machine that could, automatically and with regularity, remove the husk from the wheat. The brushes would do just that. What then was needed, he thought, was an automatic conveyance to push the wheat through, so the brushes could efficiently and effectively do their work.

Alec recalled that when they'd looked around the mill the first time, he'd seen the remains of some old farm machine, so he searched and finally found what he was looking for. It was a wooden set of rotating paddles. Alec took the junk to his worktable, where he attached the brushes, hammered the nails in, and, leaning over intently, worked efficiently and quickly, until he was satisfied.

When he was finished, he went over to one of the wheat piles and hauled it to a table. Feeding it through one end of the machine, the brushes scraped the husks off the wheat automatically, while the wooden paddles conveyed them through the device to the exit.

"It was a proud day for us when we boys marched into Mr. Herdman's office [and] presented him with our sample of cleaned wheat," Alec recalled many years later. "Herdman's injunction to do something useful was my first incentive to invention, and the method of cleaning wheat the first fruit of my efforts."[3]

But it was his sense of hearing that was Alec's real talent. He showed so much aptitude at the piano, that his parents got him lessons from Auguste Benoit Bertini, a renowned pianist. Then, when Alec was thirteen in 1860, Melville sent him to London to live with his recently widowed grandfather, Alexander Bell, also a speech teacher.

For the Bells, speech was a family business.

Shaw might have based *Pygmalion* on what happened to Alec Bell at his grandfather's in London, if he hadn't had someone else in mind. The old man had his grandson cast off his knockabout clothes and replace them with the more formal Eton jacket, top hat, and cane. Alec felt like a fop in the outfit, but what was he to do? He had to obey his grandfather.

What Grandfather Bell was really doing was taking a country boy and refining his manner of dress and speech. Simultaneously, he gave his grandson the gift of elocution lessons. And the more Alec studied speech and sound, the more fascinated he was by it.

"This period of my life seems to be a turning point of my whole career. It converted me from a boy somewhat prematurely into a man," Bell later wrote.

When Melville came to visit, he and his son went to see a demonstration of a machine called a speaking automaton. Developed by Sir Charles Wheatstone, a noted scientist, "I saw Sir Charles manipulate the machine and heard it speak and although the articulation was disappointingly crude, it made a great impression on my mind," Bell wrote later.[4]

Wheatstone had based his invention on the sound experiments of Baron Wolfgang von Kempelen, which he had laid out in a book. When he returned to Edinburgh, Alec got a copy of von Kempelen's book. It was written in German, but that didn't stop him. It took him months, but Alec finally translated the whole thing into English.

When Alec came home from London the following year—such a good graduate of his grandfather's tutelage that, forever more, people would think he was ten years older than he was because of his incredible professional polish—his father challenged Alec and his older brother, Melville James (nicknamed Melly), to create a machine that would recreate speech much more accurately than Wheatstone's method.

The boys divided up the work. Melly would make the lungs and throat, while Alec the tongue and mouth. Alec poured over books of human anatomy, but he went even further. He viewed autopsies, to see the head from the inside out. Soon, Alec constructed lifelike lips and most importantly a windpipe, to which he attached a bellows. Forcing air through the windpipe, the boys then adjusted the lips to produce real words.

They took their invention outside into the common staircase of their Charlotte Square building, where they demonstrated their invention publicly for the first time.

"Mama, mama," said the head in a clear tone.

A moment later, someone shouted down from a window above, "Good gracious, what can be the matter with that baby?"

Alec and Melly heard footsteps. Someone was running down to see if a baby was in distress.

"This of course was just what we wanted. We quietly slipped into our house, and closed the door, leaving our neighbors to pursue their fruitless quest for the baby. Our triumph and happiness were complete," Bell later remembered. "We were more interested in strange effects than with obtaining scientific accuracy."

"Many times were we discouraged and disheartened over our efforts and ready to give the whole thing up in disgust. [We learned] the importance of perseverance and sustained effort in spite of defeat."[5]

This experience of grinding out success through defeat would stand Bell in good stead two decades later, when James Garfield needed his help.

3

"I Am Greatly Perplexed on the Question of Duty"

In the spring of 1858, Crete Rudolph began teaching art in Bryan, Ohio. That summer, James Garfield showed up and proposed marriage. Crete accepted, perhaps more out of a false sense of duty rather than passion. Facetiously, she even sent him an invitation to his own wedding. As Garfield was getting accustomed to married life in staunchly Democratic Portage County, Ohio, outside political influences were about to affect the newlyweds' life.

The Democrats had flimflammed their constituents one too many times. The dynamic Republican Party felt they could take the state senate there, with a particularly strong candidate. In the summer of 1859, they held their state convention. Who were they going to nominate to win the Portage vote? A convention member rose to address the body.

"Gentlemen, I can name a man whose standing, character, ability and industry will carry the county. It is President Garfield of the Western Eclectic Institute."

It was the first time the word "president" was used before Garfield's name publicly, but not the last. People had heard of "President" Garfield of the Western Eclectic Institute. He was a man with a SOLID reputation. A natural leader, people looked up to him. And he was a respected minister for the Disciples of Christ, no less!

By unanimous acclamation, Garfield was nominated as the Republican Party nominee to the Ohio State Senate. Almost immediately, the nomination was condemned within Portage County's religious community. Garfield was a popular preacher; parishioners and elders alike were not going to sit by and lose him to politics.

In England, the star chamber was a court controlled by the monarch. It was a court that sat in name only; the verdict was known before the defendant sat on the dock. Abolished in 1641 by Parliament exactly because of that, the Disciples of Christ convened a star court of church elders, to try Garfield for his crime of going secular.

The court claimed he could not maintain his integrity, and his religious life, if he was elected to public office. Their condemnation did not matter. Despite their pressure, Garfield kept his ministerial position. He thought about the matter and then revealed his feelings in a letter to a friend: "I have wanted to enter political life. Such has been my secret ambition for some time. This nomination opens the way, I believe, for me to enter into the life work I have always preferred. I have made up my mind."

There was, however, one big obstacle: his mother.

"My success as a preacher has been a great satisfaction to her. If she will give her consent, I will accept the nomination," Garfield continued.

Twenty-eight-year-old college president James Garfield traveled to the home of his friend, Jason Robbins, in order to see his sixty-year-old mother, Eliza Ballou, who had come from their farm to meet him halfway. While Jason gave them their privacy, mother and son spoke.

"James, I have had a hope and a desire ever since you joined the church that you would preach. I have been happy in your success as a preacher, regarding it as an answer to my prayers. Of late, I regarded the matter as settled. But I do not want my wishes to lead you into a life work that you do not prefer to all others, much less the ministry, unless your heart is in it.

"If you can retain your manhood and religion in public life, and believe you can do the most good there, you have my full consent and prayers for your success. A mother's prayers and blessing be yours," Eliza Garfield told her son.

She could not keep the disappointment out of her words. Questioning his "manhood," because he was choosing an active political life in order to serve others, rather than perhaps a more

passive religious life doing the same thing, was not exactly a ringing endorsement of what her son now began to believe might
be his life's work.[1]

Garfield accepted the nomination from the Republican Party
for the Ohio State Senate and was overwhelmingly elected. Two
years later, in the winter of 1861, he was still serving in the state
senate when the telegrams began pouring in from Fort Sumter
in Charleston Harbor. It was being fired upon by the "Sechers"
(Secessionists). It took the Sechers thirty-four hours of artillery
barrage before the federal fort in Charleston Harbor surrendered.

Abraham Lincoln had been president for less than a month.
Before he'd even taken office on March 3, seven states had
already seceded from the Union, forming the Confederate States
of America. Not only did President Buchanan let them secede
without a fight, he let them take control of federal forts within
their state, without a single shot from a single federal gun.

"The South has no right to secede, but I have no power to
prevent them," Buchanan said, shortly before he departed the
White House.[2] He left the country on the brink of civil war.
When Fort Sumter was finally taken by the Sechers, on April
13, 1861, the War Between the States officially began.

The American flag with its thirty-three stars, representing the thirty-three states, was lowered. Raised in its place to
proudly wave in the harbor breeze was the Stars and Bars, the
first national flag of the Confederacy. This schism had been a
very long time coming, a path filed with negotiation, compromise, and, ultimately, war.

Eighty-five years earlier, John Adams, Thomas Jefferson, and
Benjamin Franklin had gotten the Declaration of Independence
passed, but only by striking out the section of Jefferson's original draft condemning slavery. Ever the revolutionary, Adams
had objected to its deletion. Ever the pragmatist, Franklin convinced Adams that if they didn't strike it out, the South would
not vote for independence. He was, of course, right.

Franklin figured future generations would take care of the
matter of slavery. That compromise led to two more—the Mis-

souri Compromise and the Kansas-Nebraska Act—the last allowing new states to decide for themselves, when they joined the Union, whether they would be a free state or a slave state.

James Garfield knew that the stakes of this rebellion were high—the very soul of the Union. Unless the Sechers were defeated in battle, slavery would not only survive, it would flourish, spreading to the northern and western states, and eventually to all territories.

The easy Southern victory at Fort Sumter demonstrated that the Union did not have an adequate standing army to defend itself. Moving quickly to fortify his forces, Lincoln called for the immediate, ninety-day enlistment of every able-bodied man to defend the Union. The twenty-three states remaining in the Union rapidly gathered volunteers for enlistment in Mr. Lincoln's army.

On June 14 1861, Garfield wrote to his lifelong friend, D. S. Hinsdale: "The Lieutenant-colonelcy [*sic*] of the 24th Regiment has been tendered to me and the Governor urges me to accept. I am greatly perplexed on the question of duty. I shall decide by Monday next."

After a five-year courtship, Garfield had married Lucretia Rudolph in 1858. They already had a two-year-old daughter, Eliza Arabella. Who would provide for his family if he were cut down by a Southern ball? Despite the three thousand dollars he had managed to save, Garfield was practical enough to know that his wife and child would soon be destitute if he didn't survive.

He declined the governor's generous offer. Still, his conscience bothered him.

On May 13, 1861, Dr. D. Willard Bliss left his piano and practice behind. The war had started and the Union needed him.

Already active in the state militia, Bliss volunteered for the regular army and was commissioned surgeon of the Third Regiment, Michigan Infantry. By July, Bliss's unit had marched south and then east. They were part of a thirty-five-thousand-man Union army, marching into battle at the key Southern railroad junction of Manassas, in northern Virginia.

The enlistment of the "ninety-dayers" was about to run out.

The men had been able to go through minimal training. These thirty-five thousand were an undisciplined group of individuals, not an army that knew how to fight together. Making matters worse, their commander was forty-three-year-old General Irvin McDowell.

Months before, Governor William Dennison of Ohio, McDowell's cousin by marriage, had considered making his cousin the commander of Ohio's troops. But Dennison instead went with George B. McClellan. A career army officer, McDowell was promoted at the outbreak of the rebellion. Using his political connections, he got command of the Union army, and soon was to engage the rebels.

McDowell was not a field commander; he had never led men into battle. Not surprisingly, he wasn't anxious to order this group into battle either. McDowell continued to delay mounting an attack. Simultaneously, powerful Northern newspapers called for President Lincoln to bring a quick end to the insurrection. They wanted an immediate military victory against the Southern usurpers.

Lincoln brought McDowell to the White House and told him that something needed to be done. McDowell didn't want to go into action, but he couldn't tell the president no. Thirty-five thousand troops were bivouacked around Washington. McDowell formulated a plan to march them thirty miles south and attack the Confederate garrison at Manassas, Virginia.

Manassas had a major rail line. Seizing it would disrupt the Confederacy's supply lines. The Union army expected to win this first battle. Running the Sechers back to Atlanta and Galveston Bay was a popular sentiment of the overconfident North.[3] The plan looked good in theory. But theory didn't take into consideration a poorly conditioned army, marching in woolen uniforms and with full packs in ninety-eight-degree heat and 90 percent humidity.

It was in the middle of the summer, over rutted roads. Those thirty miles took two days of forced march, during which many of the raw recruits decided to unburden themselves of the additional weight of ammunition and food. The exhausted and ill-provisioned troops finally reached their destination on Thursday, July 18, 1861.

In the twilight, the soldiers could hear a rushing stream. Moving toward the sound, through the willows, oaks, and bushes in full summer bloom, their young eyes made out through the night's descending gloom the slow stream called Bull Run. Camp was quickly set up and pickets were assigned to the perimeter. A farmhouse was commandeered as the military hospital.

Brig. Gen. Daniel Tyler's Union division skirmished with rebel troops and lost 150 men. McDowell then formulated a battle plan. However, thirty-five thousand Union troops marching south in the middle of the summer was easy to notice. In response to the Union's aggression, the Confederates were moving up reinforcements and would eventually amass an army of twenty thousand men at Manassas.

Despite their lack of numbers, the South's advantage over the Union forces was a simplistic and vastly superior one—they had already tasted blood at Fort Sumter. The Union army opposing them was callow and untested, not unlike the courier sent from Gen. Winfield Scott in Washington.

Last in his class at West Point, the twenty-one-year-old courier had just graduated from the military academy in New York's Hudson Valley. Like most of the Union troops, he had never seen battle. Riding alone down the trail into Virginia, his red bandana fluttered in the night breeze. He reached McDowell's field headquarters in Centerville, Virginia, at about 3:00 a.m.

Ushered into the general's presence, McDowell could not have failed to notice the junior officer's long lean face, framed by a heavy, drooping blond mustache. He wore a regulation officer's hat with a turned-up brim. Blond locks flowed down to his neck. He was a bit of a dandy. Maybe his flamboyance was meant to distract from his one facial imperfection—a hooked nose.

"Lieutenant George Armstrong Custer reporting, Sir, with a dispatch from General Scott," the twenty-one-year-old first lieutenant said, saluting his superior officer crisply.[4]

4

"The Men of the Third Infantry Were Not Receiving the Best of Medical Care"

Custer handed over an envelope to the old general, which contained his orders. The troops were already awake and up in anticipation. Everyone knew the battle would start that day. Aware of that fact, the gentry of Washington streamed out of the city on Sunday morning, July 21. They were curious to see what would happen in the first great engagement of the war.

On hills overlooking what would soon be the Manassas battlefield, throngs of people arrived with their picnic lunch to watch. The sun was clear and bright. The women dressed in their best, while the gentlemen were gay. They set up neat linen cloths on the ground, so they wouldn't get dirty while they ate and watched men die. It was the American version of the Roman Coliseum.

Many were expecting a rout. This untrained Union army was going to win!

Within hours, Union infantry, following the orders from Scott via Custer to McDowell, crossed Bull Run Creek, engaging the Confederates, and pushing them back, forcing the Confederate battle lines momentarily to disintegrate. Standing his ground against the white hot lead flying around him, Confederate General Thomas Jackson refused to be cowed.

Jackson organized his men and charged the Union lines. "And when you charge, yell like furies!" he said at the top of his lungs. It was the first time the fabled "Confederate yell" was used in battle. The Confederates rallied round the general forever more known as "Stonewall,'" driving the ninety-dayers back across the creek and into the woods.

As the afternoon wore on, the South began to get the upper

hand. Corporal Samuel J. English, Company D of the Second Rhode Island Volunteers, was present.

"The bodies of the dead and dying were three and four deep. In the woods, where the desperate struggle between the U.S. Marines and the Louisiana Zouaves had taken place, the trees were spattered with blood and the ground strewn with dead bodies. The shots flying pretty lively round me, I thought best to join my regiment," Corporal English later wrote in a letter to his mother.

"As I emerged from the woods, I saw a bombshell strike a man in the breast, and literally tear him to pieces. I passed the farm house, which had been appropriated for a hospital, and the groans of the wounded and dying were horrible."

Inside, D. W. Bliss was operating. Of all his medical tools, the saw came in most handy. He had noticed that the Minié balls (bullets) from the Confederate rifles flattened on impact, destroying soft tissue and shattering bones. If the subsequent wound didn't become infected, a quick amputation was the best way to save a life.

Outside the hospital tent, the Confederates were engaged in a rout. Bliss heard the rebel yells for the first time. Jackson's exhortation had worked. The Yanks became petrified by the sound. That plus the Southerners' grit shattered the Union lines, as easily as the Minié ball shattered bones. The unprepared, ill-trained, and ill-equipped Union soldiers stared as one into the raging faces of the charging Southern devils.

Frightened with the threat of imminent death, the Union army turned and ran back toward Washington, shedding what was left of their gear in their wake, so they could run faster. They were nothing more than a blue-coated mob, though some wags would later claim that their color was yellow.

Suddenly experiencing the bloody reality of war, the horrified picnickers joined the Union army's retreat. The Southerners decided not to pursue them. They were too exhausted from the day's exertions, and so chose to let the Yankees run back to their foul president with their tails between their legs.

"THE MEN OF THE THIRD INFANTRY"

Though he was but a courier, young Lieutenant Custer was ready to countercharge with the cavalry. But the cavalry troops were held back. The nascent warrior's first taste of combat consisted of watching shell bursts off to his left or right and hearing, for the first time, cannon balls whizzing over his head. As the federals fell back, Custer became part of that grand retreat and spoke almost humorously of it later on.[1]

The president, however, saw no humor in the situation. The Northern newspapers had been clamoring for a Union victory, and instead got a resounding defeat, not to mention total humiliation. Lincoln was in the same situation as General Washington at the Battle of Trenton. What was needed was a victory to shore up the Union's collective sense of confidence.

To do that, Lincoln realized, he needed a new general.

The day after the defeat at Bull Run, Lincoln told Winfield Scott to clear out his office at the War Department. He was fired. The president immediately appointed Maj. Gen. George B. McClellan to command the newly established, Army of the Potomac. He followed that by signing a bill calling for the enlistment of one million troops, whose time in blue would be three years, *not* three months.

When the numbers were added up, the Union army's dead and wounded at the Battle of Bull Run numbered almost two thousand, in but a few hours. With that kind of casualty rate, D. W. Bliss should have been very busy. However, "there had been rumors circulating around western Michigan that the men of the Third infantry were not receiving the best of medical care. It seems that certain allegations were made against [Bliss] and [his] performance during the various actions along the Bull Run in northern Virginia between July 18 and July 21, 1861."[2]

The allegations, cowardice under fire, had enough legs that Bliss needed to reply publicly before there was a chance of charges being filed. Again Bliss used the press to his advantage, or rather, his advocates did. Colonel McConnell, Lt. Col. Ambrose Stevens, Major Stephen Champlin, and Quartermaster

Robert Collins of the Third Michigan signed and sent an open letter, dated August 7, to the *Grand Rapids Enquirer*:

> Dr. D. Willard Bliss was all that day [July 18] at his proper post at the Brigade hospital, established in the rear of the line, attending to his duties as surgeon. On Sunday, the day of the last battle of Bull Run, [his] services not being required by our Regiment beyond prescribing for a few sick, which duty performed, [he was] ordered by the Surgeon General to open a hospital at Centreville, and take charge of, and prescribe for the sick, and treat such of the wounded of other Regiments as should present themselves for treatment.

But Bliss's advocates had a bit of a memory problem.

There was no "last battle of Bull Run." Prior to Sunday, July 18, 1861, there had been some minor skirmishes, but no "battle." That day, there was only one real battle between the two forces, when all the casualties took place. Then why had D. W. Bliss gone behind the lines while the battle raged? His superiors' assertion that the regiment hadn't needed his services belies historical fact.

That Sunday, 460 Union soldiers were killed and 1,124 wounded. Nevertheless, the excuse that his services weren't needed "accounts for [his] severance from the Regiment during the retreat, and for [his] arrival in Washington in advance thereof [of their Regiment]. We think that the officer who ordered them off, under the circumstances, transcended his duty, and that in complying, they had no other idea than that they were obliged to obey the order of a superior officer thus given," the letter to the *Enquirer* continued.

It was a standard operating principle, however, of the United States Army in 1861, as it is now, that if an officer disagrees on moral grounds with a superior officer's orders, such as deserting the battlefield while men are still being shot and need to be cared for, he doesn't have to obey the order. Instead, Bliss complied with his superior's order, leaving the wounded and dying on the trail behind him.

Corporal Samuel D. English writes:

The R.I. regiments, the New York 71st and the New Hampshire 2nd were drawn into a line to cover the retreat, but an
officer galloped wildly into the column crying, "the enemy
is upon us." Off they started like a flock of sheep, every man
for himself, rebels' shot and shell fell like rain among our
exhausted troops.

As we gained the cover of the woods, the stampede became
even more frightful, for the baggage wagons and ambulances
became entangled with the artillery and rendered the scene
even more dreadful than the battle. As we neared the bridge,
the rebels opened a very destructive fire upon us, mowing
down our men like grass.

Our artillery and baggage wagons became fouled with
each other, completely blocking the bridge, while the bomb-
shells bursting on the bridge made it rather unhealthy to be
around. As I crossed on my hands and knees, Capt. Smith
who was crossing by my side at the same time, was struck by
a round shot at the same time, and completely cut in two.[3]

Bliss had left all of this to get to Centreville. He was only
"following orders," his superiors attesting to that fact, in print
no less. By running, Bliss drove through the lines of men leaving wounded and dying Union soldiers he had sworn, under
oath, to serve as their departmental surgeon. Yet he showed
no remorse or guilt over his actions.

"A great battle fought. I [am] safe," Bliss wrote in a telegram
to a relative back in Michigan.[4]

• • •

Governor Dennison of Ohio remained undeterred. In championing McClellan over McDowell to take command of the Army
of the Ohio months before the war started, and almost a year
before Lincoln appointed McClellan to command the Army of
the Potomac, Dennison clearly showed his ability to judge military talent. On July 27, he again wrote to James Garfield: "I am

organizing new regiments. Can you take a lieutenant colonelcy? I am anxious you should do so. Reply by telegraph."[5]

Garfield knew that he couldn't very well turn the governor down a second time. The Union had just lost at Bull Run, and he was uncharacteristically angry. He knew he had to go. He was passionately committed to the Union, and against slavery, as much as any man could be. He was a Christian, a preacher, and he knew the Bible.

Didn't Moses lead his people out of bondage, "with a strong hand and an outstretched arm?"

Buchanan and the Democrats had set this whole thing up. Now Lincoln, the newly elected, antislavery Republican president, would be left to have to clean up the mess. He needed men like Garfield to help him. Garfield went home, told Crete what he was going to do, and then telegraphed the governor.

He would place his life on the altar of the Union, like Abraham placed Isaac's on the Lord's at Mount Moriah. He would ask the Lord to be as merciful to him as he had been to Isaac, and his father, Abraham. On August 16, 1861, James Garfield reported for duty and was given a commission as a lieutenant colonel of the Ohio volunteers.

5

"To Lose Kentucky Is Nearly the Same as to Lose the Whole Game"

Humphrey Marshall was a conflicted man. Not a good trait for a field general being asked to kill the enemy.

Marshall had a problem. Like a lot of Americans, he wondered who the enemy was. His uncle, James G. Birney, was a famous abolitionist. William and David B. Birney, his two first cousins, were both major generals in the Union army.

When the Confederate States of America was formed earlier in the year, South Carolina, Mississippi, Florida, Alabama, Georgia, Louisiana, and Texas were the first states to secede from the Union. After Lincoln called for the ninety-dayers to enlist, Virginia, Arkansas, North Carolina, and Tennessee shortly followed suit.

Kentucky, however, did something decidedly unusual. The state where Daniel Boone made his reputation was born from a little thing called territorial geography, which Kentuckians took very seriously. The state's northern border was on the Ohio River, right across from Indiana. It was as much a part of the North as it was the South. Faced with choosing sides, Kentucky became the United States' version of Switzerland—it stayed neutral.

Refusing to secede from the Union when its fellow Southern states did exactly the opposite, Kentucky now thumbed its nose in the face of the upstart, eleven-state Confederacy. That didn't sit well with Kentucky native Jefferson Davis, who had recently been elected president of the Confederate States of America.

Before the war, Humphrey Marshall had served as a Kentucky congressman. He was one of many who had advocated that Kentucky remain neutral. But once the war started, neutrality would not be tolerated. Once Fort Sumter was fired upon,

Marshall did what he felt was the honorable thing—he resigned from Congress and enlisted in the Confederate army.

A West Pointer, he had previously risen to the rank of second lieutenant during the Mexican-American War, before leaving to go into politics. Jefferson Davis commissioned Marshall as a brigadier general and put in him command of the Confederate troops stationed in western Virginia (now West Virginia).

Davis soon called for Marshall to attack Kentucky and force them into the Confederacy. Following Davis's orders, Marshall moved into Kentucky. The state's unique geography meant that the Confederates would actually have a foothold in the North, if they could successfully occupy it, and kick the Union out. However it seemed that the other president, also a Kentucky native, had an even keener appreciation of his home state's importance to the Union.

"To lose Kentucky is nearly the same as to lose the whole game. We would as well consent to separation at once, including the surrender of the capital. I hope to have God on my side, but I must have Kentucky," Lincoln wrote in a September 1861 letter to friend Orville Browning.[1]

A few months later, Louisville saw something it had never seen before—one, continuous line of paddle-wheelers chugging down the Ohio River, crowding into the city's harbor. When the steamboats docked, thousands of Union soldiers, all in blue-coated uniforms, disembarked from the splendid ships. The "green," well-drilled though untested troops marched down the gangplanks and crowded into the downtown streets, before following their officers south and into battle.

The Union general stayed behind and set up his headquarters on one of the most aristocratic streets in Louisville, Fourth Street between Green and Walnut. His name was Don Carlos Buell. The name sounded like it belonged to a wealthy, aristocratic California landowner, instead of what he was—an Ohio farm boy with brains, much like the younger man, James Garfield, whose services he had just requested.

The upcoming battle would pit the North against the South,

with the state of Kentucky as the ultimate prize. General Buell needed all the help he could get, as he was an older man. In 1861 when the average male lifespan in the United States was just under forty, Buell had reached the ripe old age of forty-two, despite his rather dangerous profession as a professional soldier.

Like Marshall, Buell was a West Pointer, who had also distinguished himself during the Mexican-American War, in the battle on the Monterrey Peninsula. The job given by General McClellan to this other Ohio boy was a simple one—drive the Confederates out of Kentucky.

After the Battle of Bull Run, Dr. D. W. Bliss had gotten leave and returned home to his family in Grand Rapids. His time spent in the Washington DC area had convinced him of the probable success of setting up a medical practice in that district. People with money lived there, like lawyers, politicians, engineers, all of whom had business with the seat of American government.

In September 1861, the army gave Bliss a promotion to major and surgeon of the United States Volunteers. He was ascending the army's ranks rapidly. In October he received his second promotion in as many months to brigade surgeon. He was transferred to the staff of Brig. Gen. Israel Richardson, who commanded the Third Division, Third Corps, to which the Third Michigan was attached.[2]

While Garfield rarely saw his siblings, Bliss had one at his side. His brother Zena, who had replaced him as the Third Michigan's regimental surgeon, tented with him while he served on Richardson's staff. It was a cushy job. While Bliss was enjoying it, on December 17, 1861, Lt. Col. James Garfield came galloping into Louisville.

The big man reined up his horse to a grand building on Fourth Street. Handing the reins to a sentry who took them and stood at attention, Garfield strolled inside with his long and steady gait. The men in his company had already gone south, bypassing Louisville, waiting in the field for his further orders. Those orders would be created by General Buell, who had summoned Garfield to his side.

In his makeshift office, Buell presented the problem to the former college president and state legislator. How was the Union army going to kick the rebels out of Kentucky? Shortly, Buell told his subordinate to retire to his quarters for the night, telling him that at promptly 9:00 a.m. the next morning, Buell expected Lt. Col. Garfield to present his plan for the military campaign to drive the Confederates out of Kentucky.

Saluting, Garfield was taken to a room in a building nearby, where he shut himself up with only a map of Kentucky and a lantern. All night, he pondered over the situation.

Humphrey Marshall, with several thousand Confederate troops, was rapidly taking possession of eastern Kentucky. Entering from Virginia through Pound Gap, he had quickly crossed Pike County into Floyd, had positioned himself close to Prestonsburg and was preparing to increase his forces and advance farther. His present situation was at the head of the Big Sandy River. Catlettsburg, where the troops of the Forty-seventh Ohio had gone, was at the head of this river.

Simultaneously, an invasion was planned from Tennessee to the south, which would be executed by Brig. Gen. Felix Zollicoffer of the Confederacy. He was advancing toward Mills Spring, intending to combine his forces with Marshall's. Accomplishing that would make the rebel influence in the state complete and unbeatable. The Kentucky legislature would have no choice but to vote secession.

In seclusion, Garfield studied the subject with tireless attention. When the day dawned, he was beginning to see the light. Promptly at 9:00 a.m., the Ohio colonel stood before his general and delivered his plan about how to chase the Confederates out of Kentucky.

A regiment was to be left in the interior of the state, near the big city of Lexington, to give the Kentuckians confidence that the Union army had everything in control. Meanwhile, Garfield would be leading his troops up the Big Sandy River, to its mouth, where he would engage Marshall's troops and run them back to Virginia.

"TO LOSE KENTUCKY"

After that, Garfield planned to turn his forces toward western Kentucky, to prevent any Confederate attack from that direction. As for the formidable Zollicoffer, he would have to be taken by a separate military expedition.

Buell listened intently, gazing at the map periodically, standing next to his young lieutenant colonel. At last, the general nodded. The campaign had been wisely planned. That evening, Garfield was in his quarters when he got his official orders from Buell:

Headquarters, Department of the Ohio, Louisville KY Dec. 17, 1861

Sir: The Brigade organized under your command is intended to operate against the rebel force threatening, and indeed actually committing, depredations in Kentucky, through the valley of the Big Sandy. The actual force of the enemy, from the best information I can gather, does not probably exceed twenty-five hundred, though rumors place it as high as seven thousand.

I can better ascertain the true state of the case when you get on the ground. Go first to Lexington and Paris, and place the regiment in such a position as will best give a moral support to the trip to Prestonburg and Piketon, and oppose any further advance of the enemy on the route.

Then proceed with the least possible delay to Sandy, and move with the force in that vicinity up that river, and drive the enemy back, or cut him off. Having done that, Piketon will probably be in the best position for you to occupy, to guard against future incursions.

Artillery will be of little, if any service to you in that country. If the enemy have any, it will incumber [sic] and weaken, rather than strengthen them.

Garfield was at a distinct disadvantage with many of his officer brethren—he had not been trained at West Point. He was a citizen soldier, who was being asked to put his money where his mouth was. On the other hand, he was a classically educated freethinker, whereas the military college taught the archaic war tactics popular since Napoleon's time, sixty years before stand-up, frontal assaults.

Yes, armaments had changed as technology advanced. They were more deadly and more accurate. To many West Point officers on each side of the conflict, human life meant nothing. Troops were expendable. Garfield didn't think that way. He would have to learn tactics as he went along. But human life was not expendable.

For him, fighting for the Union was a spiritual calling. It was quite simple: slavery was against the laws of God and man and should be abolished. The Sechers had violated the Constitution by seceding from the Union. They were federal criminals.

Garfield telegraphed his forces at Catlettsburg to march up the Big Sandy toward Marshall's advance post in Paintsville. Buell then sent James and his newly formed Fortieth Ohio recruits south through Ohio, and into the Kentucky breach. Men who just months before were teachers, blacksmiths, and storekeepers—all kinds of professions—had a new job: they were to engage Humphrey Marshall's well-trained troops at Paintsville on Painter Creek, near the west fork of the Big Sandy River, about thirty miles upriver from Louisa, Kentucky. Marshall had 3,500 troops to Garfield's 1,700. The young colonel knew he was outnumbered two to one, but figured that a quick, surprise attack would end with Marshall's retreat.

He had learned in his studies of ancient history that the Carthaginian Hannibal was the only general ever to defeat the Romans in battle. Part of the reason Hannibal ultimately lost the war was because he didn't have proper reinforcements to defeat the Roman armies. The Carthaginian Empire had therefore fallen. The point was well taken.

Garfield wrote out an order, requesting reinforcements from Colonel Jonathan Cranor, who was with the Forty-eighth Ohio, stationed at Paris, Kentucky. He gave it to Richard Paul Coppage, a scout who rode out to deliver it to Cranor.[3]

6

"I Probably Should Not Have Kept Attacking"

December 23, 1861

In subfreezing temperatures, the march to Paintsville began. The men struggled under their packs over hills slippery with ice. Two weeks later, the weather was less important. By January 5, 1862, the Fortieth Ohio had already skirmished a half-dozen times with the advancing Confederates. No one had been killed, but they had traded prisoners of war.

On the night of January 6, three interesting things occurred. The first was that Harry Brown appeared. It must have been quite a reunion. Brown was one of Garfield's old friends from his six-month canal-boat tour. Brown happened to be nearby. When he heard that his old friend from the canals was in the neighborhood, he took britches to saddle.

Appearing at Garfield's headquarters, he offered his services as a scout to his old comrade. Garfield wisely accepted. Brown quickly scouted out the territory, noting the position and strength of the Confederate force. The second thing that happened was that the scout returned with a precious dispatch from Colonel Cranor. Cranor would be arriving in two days with reinforcements.

That left the third thing, which was another dispatch. Except this time, it was captured from an enemy soldier. It was a letter from Humphrey Marshall. In it, Marshall revealed that his force was far less than the Union army had been led to believe. Inflating the numbers of his force had been meant to scare them. It was a flimflam worthy of P. T. Barnum himself, if it had worked.

Studying the map, Garfield saw that there were three ways

to enter Paintsville—from the west, the east, and the north. Marshall was sure to have put out his scouts on each road. To beat him, Garfield decided to do something completely different—he would attack not one road, as Marshall would expect, but two simultaneously. Splitting his force, Garfield dispatched a small detachment of infantry, supported by cavalry, to attack from the west.

In response, Marshall sent almost his entire force out to meet them. Simultaneously, the second and superior part of Garfield's troops attacked from the east. The Confederates literally had to stop in defense and turn midfield, in the opposite direction. Breaking through the Confederate lines, Garfield drove his men directly into the village of Paintsville, which was completely empty.

The Confederate troops were otherwise engaged behind him. Garfield had decimated the Confederate line. He drove further on, coming to a partially fortified farmhouse, which Marshall had made his headquarters. Marshall was inside, waiting for word from the field. Surmising the battle had already been lost, the not very creative Marshall had ordered his men to retreat from the farmhouse, which accounted for its partial fortifications.

Now seeing Union soldiers literally outside his window, Marshall ran frantically for the rear door. Following Marshall into the night, his army retreated across the Big Sandy River. On the other side of the river, they bivouacked for the night. A few men in the retreat were lost, but the moral blow to the Confederates was much greater.

The Union was now in control of Paintsville. The next morning brought even worse news for Marshall. Garfield and his troops were moving in their direction. Worse yet, Colonel Cranor was approaching with 3,300 reinforcements. Humphrey Marshall knew a losing hand when he held one. Burning his stores behind him, the Confederate general and his men fled toward Virginia.

But that didn't stop Garfield. He kept advancing and by January 11, almost all the Confederates were forced out of Kentucky. Unfortunately in so doing, Garfield had committed Hannibal's mistake. He had advanced too far forward. His supply lines were cut by the cold, snowy weather that made the roads impassable.

"If I had been an officer of more experience, I probably should not have kept attacking. As it was, having gone into the Army with the notion that fighting was our business, I didn't know any better," he later told an acquaintance.

Not only were the roads impassable, the boatmen thought the Big Sandy River was too high and dangerous for a steamboat to bring up supplies. But the former canal boy felt differently. Accompanied by his canal compadre Harry Brown, Garfield set off in a skiff, up the raging waters. Arriving at Catlettsburg three days later, he located a small steamer, the *Sandy Valley*, which he and Brown loaded with provisions.

Then he ordered the captain and crew to get up steam and take them back down the river to his starving troops. The captain and crew outright refused. The still-raging waters were just too dangerous to attempt passage, so Garfield went to the tiller himself. With him at the helm braving the wild torrential water, *Sandy Valley* moved like a cork through the wild and turbulent floodwaters.

The river was far out of its natural banks, rushing around a chain of hills at sharp curves. Over fifty feet deep in some places, submerged branches and trees were dangerous, waiting to tear out the ship's keel. It made no difference. For forty of the next forty-eight hours, Garfield held the wheel. Suddenly they found themselves coming to a sharp turn.

An impetuous flood of water whirled them around. Garfield tried to right the boat, as it leaned sideways and almost turned over. Sturdily and steadily, he turned the wheel, righting his ship and pulled away from the whirlpool. Soon, amid prolonged and enthusiastic cheering from the half-starved, waiting brigade, Garfield finally steered *Sandy Valley* to shore.

Garfield's hungry men unloaded the stores. As they ate, some of his men must have begun to wonder if their colonel could accomplish just about anything.

James Garfield's commander was equally as impressed. When

Garfield's report of the battle got to General Buell, he read it and replied, "The General Commanding takes occasion to thank Colonel Garfield and his troops for their successful campaign against the rebel force under General Marshall on the Big Sandy, and their gallant conduct in battle."

Lincoln's army had won. The Union had won the biggest prize of the war—the state of Kentucky. The War Department took notice of how that happened. On January 10, 1862, James Garfield was promoted to brigadier general of the Twentieth Brigade in the Army of the Ohio, which reached Shiloh, late on April 8, when the battle was over. Reduced to mop-up work, by May Garfield and his troops were on the march south, to engage the Confederates at Corinth, Mississippi.[1]

During this march, an escaped slave made his way secretly into camp. Once his presence was known to the Union soldiers, they decided to hide him. Shortly after, a bounty hunter approached, searching for the slave. He had followed the slave's trail to the Union encampment. Fuming with anger and profanity, the bounty hunter demanded that the "blue bellies" turn over the slave.

The soldiers brought the slave out of hiding. They opened his shirt, showing the scars from years of whippings, and they refused to turn him over. Fuming and threatening what he was going to do to each and every one of the blue bellies, the bounty hunter demanded to be shown to the headquarters of their commander. The Twentieth's field commander was General Thomas J. Wood.

Wood heard the bounty hunter's complaint and wrote out an order. When Garfield received it, he opened and read it disbelievingly. Wood was commanding him to make the men in his brigade, who had offered refuge to the escaped slave, surrender him up immediately to the Southern bounty hunter.

Garfield refolded the order and wrote on the back: "I respectfully, but *positively* decline to allow *my* command to search for or deliver up any fugitive slaves. I conceive that they are here for quite another purpose."

"SHOULD NOT HAVE KEPT ATTACKING"

He knew he could have been shot on the spot for refusing a superior's orders.

"Right is right, and I do not propose to mince matters at all. My soldiers are here for other purposes than hunting and returning fugitive slaves. My people on the Western Reserve of Ohio did not send my boys and myself down here to do that kind of business. They will back me up in my action."

Unlike many officers, Garfield held steadfast to his principles. Not only was Garfield not court-martialed, but Secretary of War Edwin Stanton agreed with him. A general order was issued that prevented Union soldiers from offering up escaped slaves to Southern bounty hunters.[2] As for Corinth, learning from Bull Run, and this time with Gen. Ulysses Grant commanding, the Union army approached the key Confederate rail junction cautiously, fortifying positions as they went.

Grant's actions led the town's citizens to desert the place, along with their defenders in the gray uniforms. With nothing more to do there, the Army of the Ohio was then ordered to Chattanooga. It was the second time in a row that Garfield had missed out on the action. And once he got to Tennessee, the army assigned him not to battle but to engineering.

Garfield was ordered to rebuild the war-damaged Memphis and Chattanooga Railroad. Garfield used his intellect and skill to reconstruct the railroad, trestles included, over which the Union army would speed its supplies to soldiers on the front lines. True to form, he pitched in with his men. That's what they loved about him.

Only this time, the workload was too much. The fair Ohio boy was not used to working under the hot Southern sun. Worse, his overexertion produced an attack of malaria. Though no one knew it yet, the disease came from infected mosquitoes. The conditions were ideal for his disease to again come out of hibernation.

Garfield shook, his temperature rose, his head ached and he sweated profusely. For a change, he took care of himself. He requested and was granted sick leave. On the same railroad he had just helped to reconstruct, Garfield rode north in a passenger coach, headed home to his wife, Crete, and his two-year-old daughter, Eliza, in Ohio, and some much needed rest.

At least, that's what he figured. While he had been away fighting for the Union, and without his knowledge, Garfield had been nominated by the state Republican Party for his district's congressional seat. Recuperating at his home, Garfield refused to campaign for himself. This was a pattern that would repeat itself throughout his life. He never went looking for an office; it always found him.

The last thing anyone would ever accuse James Garfield of was hubris. And, to make matters worse, he won the October election. Now what? he wondered. When he found out that he had won, the last thing Garfield was thinking about was politics. He might now be an elected congressman, but he was still first and foremost his father's son.

Abram Garfield had given his life to save his neighbors. What about the lives of his men? Who would lead them? For James Garfield, the decision was simple. How could he serve the Union best? Garfield believed that the only way to win the war was on the battlefield. It would take an intellectual equal, of which there were few, to change his position.

Meanwhile, D. W. Bliss was moving around. And up.

He was in charge of the division hospital at Savage Station, Virginia, during the Battle of Seven Pines, where 790 Union soldiers were killed and 3,594 wounded. Allen Ripley Foote was one of them. When Bliss got him on his operating table, he looked down at a man who was five feet four inches tall, with blue eyes, brown hair, and a light complexion. He was twenty years old.

"I was on my knees in the front rank," Foote wrote later, during a Confederate charge. "The corporal on my left was shot in the head, and fell across my legs. He spoke to me. I turned to look at him and said, 'I cannot stop work now to help you.'"

Just as Foote said this, he was shot, the bullet entering squarely into his breast, cutting off the first shirt button below the collar. It passed through the bone, which turned its course to the right, and passed out between the ribs.

"I was in the act of loading my gun at its muzzle. I had the powder in. When hit, my right arm fell. I tried three times to put the bullet in and finish loading, hoping to give the enemy one more shot. Finding I could not do it, I dropped my gun, unstrapped my cartridge box and crawled to the rear, until I came to a cleared field, where a battery was stationed, firing over the heads of our men into the Confederate ranks."

It wasn't until the next morning that Allen Foote was taken to the division hospital at Savage Station, Virginia, where Bliss made ready to treat him. Bliss was cutting off Allen's shirt when the enlisted man looked up at him.

"Doctor, here is a wound you cannot amputate," he said dryly.

By then Bliss had uncovered the dirty bandages and saw the gaping wound.

"It would be much better for you, my boy, if I could," the doctor said grimly.

Since Foote would not die until 1921, it is safe to say that Bliss misdiagnosed him. But President Lincoln did not have the benefit of twenty-twenty hindsight. Shortly after treating Foote, Bliss was summoned to the White House.[3]

7

"Why Don't You Plant Flower Seeds?"

Zachariah Chandler helped form the Republican Party in 1854. Three years later, he was elected to the U.S. Senate from Michigan. After the war started, he helped to raise and equip the Michigan Volunteers. A frequent visitor to the White House and a recipient of its occupant's patronage, he undoubtedly knew D. W. Bliss and recommended him to Lincoln for the job the president had in mind. The president was looking for somebody to help him organize a better system of veterans hospitals in the Washington DC area.

Since no charges were ever filed against Bliss for his conduct at Bull Run, it is highly doubtful that Lincoln knew about it. Instead, he had evidently heard only good things about Bliss from Chandler, and thus the summons to the White House.

When he got there, Bliss was asked by his commander in chief for assistance in building veterans hospitals to treat the wounded and dying. Bliss hastily agreed. Lincoln himself oversaw the building of Armory Square Hospital on the Mall, where Bliss was immediately appointed hospital superintendent.

The jerry-rigged complex would eventually house a thousand beds in twelve pavilions and overflow tents, officer quarters, service facilities, and chapel, all spread out across the green grass of the National Mall at Independence Avenue and Seventh Street. By July 1862, Armory Square Hospital was in operation.

Wounded Union soldiers were being evacuated from the Virginia battlefields onto boats that brought them to the wharves in southwest Washington. There, waiting horse-drawn ambulances rushed them through the streets of Washington, with horseshoes sending up sparks against cobblestones as they rounded the corners, hard, on their way to Armory Square Hospital.

In one of those ambulances was Allen Foote.

"In going through Washington we passed by the Armory Square Hospital, then in charge of Dr. Bliss. I 'fell out' and went into his office. Fortunately I found him at his desk," Foote later wrote.

Bliss recognized him as one of the Michigan men with whom he had served.

"See here, young man, this will never do. You will ruin my reputation. I reported you mortally wounded at Fair Oaks, and have had you dead and buried in the Chickahominy Swamp for six months," Bliss told him.

"I will improve your reputation by giving you an opportunity to resurrect me," Foote answered drily. "I do not want to be a condemned Yankee. Please find a way to save me from going to the Invalid Camp."

The latter was a place where wounded soldiers saw limited duty, and Foote wanted to go back into combat. But Bliss "immediately called the hospital steward, and ordered him to put Foote in a bed and keep him there for four days."

"I am perfectly able to be about," Foote protested. Then he added, "The Doctor said to me in an undertone, 'You stay in bed four days. By that time I will have an order reassigning you to do duty in my office.'"[1]

Bliss didn't get it. He had put the fix in for a soldier who wanted to be in combat. Instead, Foote was put in charge of issuing discharge papers to the lucky men who got out of the hospital alive. Armory Square's mortality rate was high.[2] Walt Whitman, the forty-three-year-old poet, volunteered daily at many army hospitals set up in the DC area, but was at Armory Square the most.

It was here on the Mall, within sight of the White House, that the most severely wounded were treated. Whitman kept a diary of what he found there:

Visited Armory-square hospital, went pretty thoroughly through. One young New York man with a bright handsome face had been lying for several months from a most disagreeable wound, received at Bull Run. A bullet had shot him right through the bladder, hitching him front, low in the belly, and coming out back. He had suffered much. The water came out of the wound, by slow but steady quantities.

For many weeks so that he lay almost constantly in a puddle and there were other disagreeable circumstances. He was of good heart however, At present comparatively comfortable, had a bad throat was delighted with a stick of horehound candy I gave him, with in or two other trifles.

Wednesday, February 4th.—Visited Armory-square hospital, went pretty thoroughly through wards E and D. Supplied paper and envelopes to all who wish's [sic]—as usual, found plenty of men who needed those articles. Wrote letters. Saw and talk'd with two or three members of the Brooklyn 14th regt.

A Brooklyn native, Whitman carried a haversack loaded with stuff the wounded soldiers needed and the government didn't have any money to pay for—crackers, peaches, preserves, tea, oysters, tobacco, brandy, stamps, envelopes and note paper, fresh underwear and handkerchiefs, socks, and the morning papers. He had raised the necessary funds for these luxuries from private sources.

A poor fellow in ward D, with a fearful wound in a fearful condition, was having some loose splinters of bone taken from the neighborhood of the wound. The operation was long and one of great pain yet, after it was well commenced, the soldier bore it in silence. He sat propp'd up, and was much wasted.

He had lain [sic] a long time quiet in one position, not for days but weeks; a bloodless brown-skinn'd face with eyes full of determination. There was an unusual cluster of surgeons, medical cadets and nurses around his bed. I thought the whole thing was done with tenderness and done well.

"WHY DON'T YOU PLANT FLOWER SEEDS?"

I liked the woman nurse in ward E. I noticed how she sat a long time by a poor fellow, who just had, that morning, in addition to his other sickness, bad hemorrhage. She gently assisted him; reliev'd him of the blood, holding a cloth to his mouth, as he coughed it up. He was so weak he could only just turn his head over on the pillow.[3]

A mere half-mile walk from the White House, occupied by a chief executive whose stamina was legendary, Armory Square saw frequent visits by President Lincoln.

"I see the President almost every day," Whitman wrote in his diary. "We have got so that we exchange bows and very cordial ones."[4]

The waiting faces of the injured looked up as Lincoln, the six-foot-four, rail-splitting giant, strode gingerly through their midst, the bunions on his long, thin size-twelve feet aching. His left eye drooped slightly.

"As for the President's appearance," Whitman wrote, "he has a face like a Hoosier Michelangelo so awful ugly, it becomes beautiful with its strange mouth. He has deep cut criss-cross lines, and a doughnut complexion."

Minus the doughnut, Whitman's description of Lincoln's appearance is an almost textbook definition of Marfan's syndrome, a rare genetic abnormality that would not become known until the twentieth century. It is characterized by long, loose limbs and other abnormalities, including the drooping eye, all of which Lincoln had.

When he'd finally made his way through the wards, Lincoln eventually knocked on the door of Bliss's office. He would answer the president's knock. Here D. W. Bliss held court. It was in Bliss's office that the president handed him some of his own money to help defray the doctor's expenses.

For a long time, Lincoln met Bliss twice each week to consider "the ingenious appliances" that the doctor had devised to aid in caring for and treating the wounded. The president paid for some of these appliances out of his own pocket. Unfortunately, the president paid for nothing. Bliss was as failed an inventor as Alexander Graham Bell would become a great one.

There is no record of any of Bliss's medical inventions ever working, nor of any patents in his name in the U.S. Bureau of Patents. But that didn't stop him from continuing to try. He would even try one out on James Garfield when he got the chance.

Lincoln, however, was a thrifty and practical man. He wasn't one to help defray anyone's cost without getting something back in return. The president always had a suggestion to make for the comfort of his troops.

"Why don't you plant flower seeds?" Lincoln asked Bliss one day.

Lincoln had a tenor's high-pitched voice. Uncontrolled, it was shrill. Controlled, with the power of the office he knew it was just his fate to temporarily occupy, it became a powerful political instrument that could reach the rafters.

"I would if I had seed," Bliss replied.

"I'll order them for you from the Agriculture Department."[5]

Sure enough, Lincoln did order them, and thereafter, each of the hospital's long barracks stretching out onto the Mall had ivy blooming all spring and summer long. Bliss must have enjoyed that, but not as much as he would his visit with Mr. Kingsland.

December 31, 1862

Julius Garesché was a Frenchman from Havana who became an American.

His distinguished French parents had immigrated to the United States, where his father became a diplomat. It was while his father was serving in the American diplomatic corps in Havana that Garesché was born there in 1821. A decade later, his family came back to the United States to live.

By his teens, Garesché had decided on a military career. His parents got their congressman to appoint him to West Point, where he became good friends with William Rosecrans, who was one year ahead of him. By dusk on December 31, 1862, Garesché was forty-one years old, a much respected, devout Catholic career soldier, with the rank of lieutenant colonel.[6]

His friend Rosecrans was the general commanding the Army of the Cumberland. Garesché was his chief of staff. That day, at the Battle of Stones River in Tennessee, the tide of battle turned against the Union. Devoted to his friend, Garesché accompanied Rosecrans onto the front line to turn it against an enemy attack. A Confederate canon ball came whistling by Rosecrans's head.

A moment later, the general looked over to see Garesché, astride his cantering horse. The canon ball that had missed Rosecrans had decapitated his chief of staff. But unlike his namesake in Washington Irving's 1832 short story, "The Legend of Sleepy Hollow," this headless horseman was not a Hessian ghost, but a man of flesh and blood.[7]

With blood still pumping up from his neck into the space where his head had been, Garesché fell from the saddle to the rough ground, where he bled out. The battle, though, was not over; there was no time to stop. His heart heavy at the loss, Rosecrans rode on, to continue delivering orders. It wasn't until after dusk, when the battle was over, that another of Garesché's West Point classmates, Brig. Gen. William S. Hazen, went back to search for his body.

"I chanced to pass the spot where he lay. I saw but a headless trunk. An eddy of crimson foam had issued where his head should be. He was alone, no soldier—dead nor living—near him. I at once recognized his figure. It lay so naturally, his right hand across his breast. As I approached, dismounted, and bent over him, the contraction of a muscle extended the hand slowly and slightly towards me," Hazen said.

He was able to take off Garesché's West Point class ring from his finger before rigor mortis set in. Searching his tunic, Hazen took the devotional from his pocket. Then he got some soldiers to help him dig a shallow battlefield grave.[8] That, of course, meant that Rosecrans had a critical vacancy. Who would be his next chief of staff? Who could possibly replace Garesché?

Not only was he a terrific soldier, Garesché had been a devout

Catholic, who had given Rosecrans himself lessons on Catholicism prior to the general's conversion. Because of his religious devotion, Rosecrans's desire was to have a Catholic replace a Catholic.

God forbid a Protestant.

In late April of 1863, Walt Whitman saw two officers with swords and pistols by their sides, from the army's Judge Advocate General's Corp. They were knocking at the door of D. W. Bliss's office. Bliss opened the door and they went in. It doesn't take long to say, "You are under arrest." Moments later Bliss was led over the wood-paneled threshold, an officer on each side of him, linking arms through his and directing his movements.

Days earlier, on April 24, Inspector A. C. Hamilton had issued a "Report of Investigation Against Surgeon Dr. D. Willard Bliss." In his report, Hamilton recommended that Bliss be removed from his command, "for allegedly accepting a $500 bribe, received for recommending the introduction into the hospital of a stove invented by Mr. Kingsland."[9]

The office of the Judge Advocate General had enough evidence to indict Bliss on the charge.

"Dr. D. Willard Bliss was removed from Armory [Square Hospital] and put into the Old Capitol prison," Whitman wrote a friend.[10] Bliss was following in a great man's footsteps, literally.

Months earlier, John Singleton Mosby, a Confederate cavalry officer, had occupied a cell in the Old Capital Prison. He'd been caught spying in Virginia. A Southerner who did not want to secede, he only served ten days and was treated well. Exchanged in a prisoner swap, he never forgot the Union's generosity, even when he later became the living legend known as the Gray Ghost.

As Mosby had, D. W. Bliss stared out through the bars in the window of his cell, only he was looking at his own home. When he moved his family to Washington, he got a house right off the Mall. It was a block away, but it must have felt like a thousand miles. This time, he was in real trouble, and he knew it. Bliss knew he was facing court-martial and imprisonment. How could he save himself from ruin?

8

"It Will Indeed Be a Day of Blood"

D. W. Bliss had already begun socializing in Washington circles. His contacts had brought him in touch with a man he thought could help him—John P. Hale. Hale was a Republican senator from New Hampshire, who had once been a Democrat. A self-righteous abolitionist, he was a political gadfly who saved his personal enmity for Gideon Welles, the secretary of the navy.

Hale was the chairman of the Senate Committee on Naval Affairs. He and Welles hated each other; they had a notorious feud going. Knowing Hale's disdain for the military, Bliss approached him to request his help as defense counsel. Hale accepted his case and "assisted him [Bliss], as friend and counsel, at his trial, and ultimately recommended that he should be restored to his position, cleared of the charges on June 2, and reinstated to his command of Armory Square."[1]

And that's what happened. By late that summer, Bliss's latest problems with the army had once again been buried. Only this time, it had been done by the private intervention of a United States senator. His reinstatement was cause for celebration at Armory Square Hospital, where on August 11, Whitman wrote in his diary:

> Dr. Willard Bliss was presented by the doctors under his command with a set of surgical instruments. The presentation to Dr. Bliss came off last Saturday evening in Ward F. The beds were all cleared out, the sick put in other wards, the room cleaned, hung with greens, etc., looked very nice. The instruments were there on exhibition in the afternoon.
>
> I took a view of them. They were in four cases, and looked

very fine. The formal presentation was made in the evening with speeches made by one & another. There was a band of music and good food to eat.[2]

Among others, Charles Leale was there. A twenty-three-year-old native of Yonkers, New York, he was the surgeon in charge of the Wounded Commissioned Officers' Ward. As for Whitman's judgment about Bliss, "I thought Doctor Bliss was a very fine operating surgeon. Sometimes, he performs several amputations or other operations of importance in a day. Amputations, blood, death are nothing here."

Whitman seemed more impressed by the volume of patients Bliss worked on than the patients' mortality rate. However, by then, Whitman had become close friends with Bliss, which might have affected his judgment.[3]

Soon after his party, Bliss and his wife, Sophia, left for three weeks of furlough to New York City, to take in the theater. While D. W. and Sophia were watching Edwin Booth on stage in *Hamlet*, back in DC, the extent of Hale's corruption had leaked, as reported by the Sacramento Daily Union: "Considerable astonishment has pervaded our political circles here, at the painful rumor that Senator Hale of New Hampshire has been implicated in a disgraceful transaction, of which the gist is that he has received money for services rendered, in procuring the release of a swindling Government contractor, or pseudo contractor, from the Old Capitol prison."

Taking to the floor of the Senate to defend himself against this "rumor," Hale actually authenticated it. "[I had] been called upon to defend *two* persons against charges preferred against them by the Government. The first was that of Dr. Bliss, of the Armory Square hospital." He then detailed his work on Bliss's behalf.[4]

The second client was a government contractor named Hunt, charged with defrauding the government. Hunt was superintendent of government transports at Fortress Monroe, where he made a lot of money in shady deals. Hale got Hunt released before a prosecution could begin. In both cases, Hale did not feel that accepting money from clients had compromised his office.

But Secretary of the Navy Gideon Welles wrote in his diary: "This loud mouth paragon, whose boisterous professions of purity, and whose immense indignation against a corrupt world were so great that he delighted to misrepresent and belie them, in order that his virtuous light might shine distinctly, is beginning to be exposed and rightly understood. But the whole is not told and never will be—he is a mass of corruption."[5]

It must have felt really good for Welles to get back at the guy who had made his life a living hell. And Bliss? He went back to business at Armory Square Hospital. After all, he wasn't the story; Hale was.

• • •

After doing practically nothing at Corinth, General Rosecrans turned the Army of the Cumberland southeast, all sixty thousand men. Obstinate, with a violent temper, he did know talent, which is why he agreed with Secretary of War Edwin Stanton's "suggestion" that James Garfield replace the late, lamented Garesché as his aide de camp (his executive officer).

Yes, Rosecrans knew Garfield was a Protestant, a Disciple of Christ, and a preacher no less. But he also knew of his burgeoning military reputation. For his part, Garfield knew that if he accepted the position—and at his level of rank, it was a choice—he could show no ego. He would actually do all the planning and implementation of military strategy, while Rosecrans would get credit for it.

Of course, Garfield readily accepted the position. The idea, now, was to capture the city of Chattanooga in southern Tennessee. It was a vital rail junction for the Confederacy. Capturing, or destroying it, would be a crippling blow to the Sechers. But marching through Georgia in the summer was even worse than marching through Mississippi months earlier.

There was heat, humidity, mosquitoes, and a civilian population not particularly fond of blue bellies. All of it wore down the Union troops, but not Confederate General Braxton Bragg. A native of North Carolina, Bragg's father had been a carpenter, just like Abram Garfield. A West Pointer, he commanded the Confederate Army of Tennessee.[6]

Bragg had a long, mournful face. But it's doubtful he looked downcast when his intelligence officers reported that the Union army, which had been marching in three separate wings, was going to unite two of them at Chickamauga Creek.[7] Bragg's plan was to cross Chickamauga Creek and attack Rosecrans and his men southwestward toward the Georgia mountains, thus stopping their advance to Chattanooga.

September 18, 1863

The cabin in the clearing reminded Garfield of home. It was the centerpiece of a small subsistence farm. The poverty that he knew the inhabitants lived under was nothing new to him. Garfield had only recently escaped from the same life, except in Ohio.

Scouts had already told him of the log cabin in the clearing. He and Rosecrans would set up their headquarters there for the impending battle. Garfield dismounted and looked around. He saw that he was in the middle of a forest, not unlike the one he grew up in. But the Georgia countryside was much different than the level Ohio countryside.

The area was dotted with fields and valleys. Garfield's keen mind immediately saw that the fractured landscape made enemy troops easily concealable. Enemy troops could be lurking around the next bend in the road, or the gully on the right.

The farm he was on belonged to a woman known as the Widow Glenn. She lived with her three children—a teenage boy, his young sister, and even younger brother—in the small cabin. When he was introduced to them, Garfield thought of his hard-working mother, brother, and sisters. Within hours, the serenity of the valley was to be shattered by the roar of drums and earth-shaking booms of cannon.

The Battle of Chickamauga had begun. All day, couriers came

in and out of the cabin, reporting to Garfield with information from the field. Garfield would read the reports, consult his maps on a table in front of him, write out a response, and then go back to moving his pins around on the map to represent his and the Confederate forces.

By the end of that first day of battle, neither force had succeeded in doing anything other than losing many men. On the morning of September 20, Garfield saw the fog, dense over of the Chickamauga River from the cabin window, mixing with the smoke of battle from the previous day that the stagnant winds had not yet dissipated. The rising sun cut through the fog of war.

"It is ominous. It will indeed be a day of blood," Garfield considered.

By nine o'clock in the morning, the fog had lifted sufficiently for the Confederates to mount an attack on the Union positions.

Like the day before, the Confederate troops began on the left, attacking General George Thomas's position, and then rolling down the line. Thomas withstood the furious assault of the enemy, who seemed to have a constant stream of reinforcements. Likewise, the demands reaching the Widow Glenn's cabin for Union reinforcements came faster and faster. Garfield moved division after division to the left.

By ten o'clock, the Army of the Cumberland was still holding the line, but how much longer they could hold in the face of such an overwhelming force was anyone's guess. And Garfield did not like guessing. He looked at war as an applied science. Everything was telling him that while no blunders had yet been made, it was just a matter of time before something went wrong.

It was impossible to do everything right during a battle, and he couldn't control everything. That included his bladder. While Garfield went out back to heed nature's call, General Rosecrans came over to take his place. An anxious courier came into the cabin with a dispatch. When Rosecrans opened it, he read that there was a chasm in the center of the line between the divisions of Generals Reynolds and Wood.

Rather than wait for Garfield to return from the outhouse,

Rosecrans stepped willingly into the breach. He wrote out an order as follows:

Brigadier General Wood, Commanding Division:

The general commanding directs that you close the gap in the line by moving to your left as fast as possible to support Reynolds.

Respectfully etc.,
General of the Army William Starke Rosecrans

Moments later, Garfield returned and Rosecrans retreated. Garfield immediately noticed that Rosecrans had changed the pins on his map. At that moment, he must have prayed to his God. Rosecrans had moved the troops in his absence. Wood was no longer next to Reynolds! A division of Confederate sharpshooters was in the line between them. A terrible mistake had been made.

Sure enough, on receipt of Rosecrans's orders, Wood was totally confused. How could he get close up to Reynolds with the Confederate sharpshooters in the way? Wood figured that Reynolds was heavily pressed and that regardless of the words in the order, its intent was to reinforce his friend.

Wood was a good soldier, who knew the importance of obeying his superior's orders. In order to prevent the army from getting tangled in the forest, he moved his division *backward*, passing to the rear of Brannon to support Reynolds. As Wood did this, the enemy was simultaneously advancing. Seeing that failure had been the only achievement on attacking Thomas to the left, the Confederates advanced all along the line.

Opposite the hole left by Wood was James Longstreet, the most desperate and fierce fighter the Confederacy had in its general command. Longstreet commanded seventeen thousand veteran troops that had fought under the personal supervision of Robert E. Lee. Formed up in one unified, solid column three-quarters of a mile long, this leviathan of an army marched into the breach.

Two brigades of Union troops advanced to meet them, only to literally be slaughtered by Longstreet's rebels. Through the gap the Confederates came, effectively splitting the Army of the Cumberland in two. Within minutes, the entire right wing was routed. Just like at Bull Run, the Union troops dropped knapsacks, blankets, anything that would impede their retreat. With Confederate bullets whizzing by their heads, they ran.

When Garfield looked out the window of the Widow Glenn's cabin, he saw a stream of fugitive soldiers, swarming back to the woods, making their way into the clearing where the cabin stood, which was a sudden and silent monument to the futility of war. Behind them came the iron columns of the enemy. In minutes, they would be at the cabin.

As soldiers around him began to frantically pack up the maps and charts, their knapsacks and personal belongings, Garfield looked out the window again. Now, the Union army was in a full rout, running by the cabin like it was just some way station in the middle of no place, instead of what it had been moments before—the headquarters of the Army of the Cumberland, which was now in shambles and in danger of destruction.

What Garfield said to the Widow Glenn and her children when he left is unknown. Yet he must have felt terrible, because the farm and the land around it were in shambles because of the battle. But he knew the widow and her kids would be safe. After all, it was their army doing the routing, and they were Southerners too.

Garfield pulled the reins, turning his horse down the Dry Valley Road over which Rosecrans had already retreated. When he was a mile away from the cabin, and still on the road, with soldiers afoot streaming by him, he reined up, determined at least to try to stop the rout physically. Snatching a flag from a color bearer that was nearby, he shouted at his men, "Hold your ground!" waving the flag as he did.

His words fell on ears deafened by the roar of the cannon, by nerves frayed by bullets whizzing by their heads. It was a mob, with a mob's thoughts, which as one were of survival. Garfield seized soldiers by their shoulders, turning them around to face the rebels and their bloodcurdling yells. His idea was to form a nucleus to resist the flood of fear, but it was to no avail. The moment Garfield removed his hands from his soldiers' torsos, they ran.

Seeing the futility of the situation, Garfield mounted and spurred his horse on, determined to catch up with Rosecrans and plan some strategy to stem what now seemed to be the inevitable tide of defeat. He finally caught up to Rosecrans who with his head start had gotten far ahead. Their horses next to each other, Rosecrans leaned over. He was his usual, blunt self.

"Garfield, what can be done?"

"One of us needs to go to Chattanooga to secure the bridges in case of total defeat and collect the fragments of the army on a new defensive line. The other, if possible, should make his way to Thomas and tell him to hold his ground at any cost until the army can be rallied at Chattanooga," Garfield replied.

"Which will you do?" Rosecrans wondered.[8]

"IT WILL INDEED BE A DAY OF BLOOD"

9

"The Republican Majority in Congress Is Very Small"

"Let me go to the front," Garfield answered. "It is dangerous, but the army and country can better afford for me to be killed than you. "

They dismounted. Using an old Indian trick, Rosecrans put his ear to the ground, listening for the sound of Thomas's guns. Garfield followed suit.

"It's no use, Garfield," he finally said, standing upright. "The fire is broken and irregular. Thomas is driven. Let us both hurry to Chattanooga to save what can be saved."

"You are mistaken," Garfield said flatly. "The fire is still in regular volleys. Thomas holds his own. As we agreed, he must be informed of the situation. Send orders to Sheridan and the other commanders of the right wing to collect the fragments of their commands and move them through Rossville and back on the Lafayette Road to Thomas's support."

The two generals mounted, shook hands, and took off in opposite directions. Rosecrans was convinced he would never see Garfield again, at least not in this life. But Garfield's thoughts were not on dying. No one knew the situation of the troops, the cause of the rout, and the way to stop it better than Rosecrans's executive officer.

On Garfield galloped, up the Dry Valley Road, parallel with the morning's line of battle. Reaching a point opposite a rise, over which he thought to find Thomas and his men, Garfield prepared to ride up it. But James Longstreet had had other ideas. After passing through the Union army's center, Longstreet had turned to the right at the Widow Glenn's cabin, marching to Thomas's rear.

Longstreet was now attacking from that angle, directly parallel with the road, along which James Garfield was in a full headlong gallop. Time after time, Garfield tried to turn toward Thomas, only to find the enemy between him and the man he was hoping to contact. If he made it, and Thomas could cover the retreat, the Army of the Potomac would be saved.

If not, and it was completely routed, that would only leave the Army of the Cumberland to do battle with the Confederacy. Garfield knew that would not be enough, and the Confederacy would be triumphant. What had begun as a simple battle had become the future of the Union.

Garfield realized that it was now or never. He needed to try to cross the valley immediately. Otherwise, the battle, and perhaps the war, would be lost. Turning sharply to his left, he soon found himself in a dark forest. The brier thickets and overhanging branches nipped at his exposed skin. Soon his face and hands were scratched and bleeding.

He ignored both, not feeling any pain because so much adrenaline was pumping through his powerful body. Making his way into a clearing, he spurred his horse to a desperate gallop. Through ravines and more forest, through impenetrable undergrowth that would have stopped a less determined man, Garfield pressed on, his horse steaming foam from overexertion.

Suddenly, he came upon a pest hut, occupied by Confederate soldiers in various stages of smallpox, a deadly disease that ravaged the planet. Languishing about this lonely place, their faces ravaged beyond recognition by the pox, the poor wretches waited for death to release them from pain. Despite the danger—they were still Confederates and had guns—and despite his urgent mission, Garfield reined up.

"Can I do anything for you, my poor fellow?" he called to the man nearest him.

The man, whose face was covered with open and oozing pustules, looked up at the vigorous Yankee general in the saddle.

"Do not come near. It is smallpox. But for God's sake, give us money to buy food."

Garfield reached into his tunic and came out with his purse, which he tossed over.

"Good-bye," he shouted and spurred his horse on toward the enemy line.

His horse dashed through the forest, the briers and branches still stinging his face and hands. Garfield stopped twice to listen for the roar of the battle. Then he stopped a third time. He looked out and, above a ridge, he heard shouting and smelled the gun smoke. The great roar of the cannons shook the ground. Men shouted, some in triumph and some, he knew, in death.

What Garfield did not know was that the rebel column had passed completely to Thomas's rear and was right in front of him. Abruptly, he wheeled toward the left, to a high ridge, over which he now knew was deadly danger. Garfield's thoughts were of Thomas and the wife and child he had left back in Hiram, Ohio. Thomas, too, hailed from the Buckeye State.

Garfield climbed the ridge and gazed down on Longstreet's troops. He realized he would have to ride through them to have any chance of reaching Thomas. Without hesitating, he spurred his horse down and into the Confederate tinder box. Two balls hit his horse with a splat, but the animal kept up its heroic ride. Garfield held to the reins with a cast-iron grip and bent as low as he could in the saddle, so as not to provide an easy target.

Garfield kept the horse in a frantic gallop. The bullets fired at him miraculously went around him, though more than once he felt a tug at his coat. With a great leap over a barricade of trees, his horse landed in the Union lines. He kept going until he found Thomas on a knoll overlooking the field of battle. Garfield's horse dropped dead just as he climbed down from its saddle. But there was no time to mourn the animal.

Most of the surviving men had already moved toward the center of the line, swinging like a door to oppose Longstreet's advance. Thomas's men had been fighting a superior force for hours. Even as the survivors fought valiantly on, corpses littered the field. The problem, Thomas realized, was that he had no plan, a problem he immediately decided to remedy.

"Withdraw!" Thomas shouted.

Buglers sounded retreat. The bedraggled survivors, twenty-five thousand out of thirty-one thousand that had taken the field the day before, followed their mounted general onto a ridge on the left, where he formed them into a horseshoe, allowing maximum firepower in each direction. Around the horseshoe, the Confederate army of sixty thousand troops pounded them with their artillery and rifles.

Beyond was the Rossville Road, where what was left of the Army of the Potomac was retreating under General Rosecrans's command. Again and again, Longstreet's men charged. By now, Garfield was with his men. Time and again, the Southerners seemed to swallow up the Union blue in a sea of Confederate gray.

At 4:30 in the afternoon, Longstreet hurled forward his reserve corps, fresh troops to the Union's, who were bloody, torn, and weary. Yet the line held.

"George A. Thomas was indeed the rock of Chickamauga against which the wild waves of battle dashed in vain," Garfield later told a newspaper reporter who asked him about that day.

Sensing he had met his match and further action would indeed be futile, Longstreet ordered his men to withdraw. As they did, Garfield held fire and looked around him. Scattered all about were thousands upon thousands of dead rebels. But there were still concerns.

Garfield surveyed the men on the ridge and found their ammunition running dangerously low. The Confederates had, many hours before, broken the Union supply lines, leaving the remaining soldiers with only the bullets in their holsters and guns.

However, Thomas had done such a good job of resisting them that Longstreet was not thinking about a counterattack, but about saving his men. Had he known the Army of the Potomac had literally run out of bullets, he certainly would have counterattacked. But he didn't know, and so Thomas's men prevailed.

As night overtook day, even the sky favored the Union. The new moon had passed and in its place was a cloudy, dark sky that covered the retreat of the survivors of the Battle of Chickamauga. They rode and walked in a column strung out for miles over the Rossville Road. Back in Chattanooga, Rosecrans did not know any of this.

No commander in the history of the republic had ever yet lost an entire command. But waiting in Chattanooga with growing dread in his heart, Rosecrans wondered how he would explain to Grant how he had lost an entire army. Making matters worse, he and Grant—still yet another Ohio general—disliked each other over some old slight going back to their days together at West Point. Rosecrans was not looking forward to his old enemy's, alcohol-fueled temper.

Then he heard it. It was a low sound at first, of horses clip-clopping, coming from the distance. It got louder and louder. Rosecrans must have been elated when he saw, materializing on his horizon, the remnants of his Army of the Potomac. A column of twenty-five thousand survivors was streaming into Chattanooga. The ones on horseback dismounted; the ones on foot just collapsed.

Some were embraced by their friends, and the wounded were taken off in stretchers to the surgeons' tents. Those who had died during the retreat went to their graves, or would when their bodies were recovered along the road. Garfield thought about what had just transpired. He had faced death before in battle, but it was not as immediate as it had been today.

Instead of the debilitating grief he thought he would feel over the dead, he felt very much alive. The grief was there all right, but the appreciation of life, and what he could accomplish with it, lifted his spirits. In later years, he thought that his life really began on the second day of the epic battle.

Garfield knew how lucky he was not to have stopped a bullet.

The Battle of Chickamauga lost the Union sixteen thousand dead and wounded. The military brass in Washington, already peeved at Rosecrans for his egotistical preening, were mortified by the casualties. With such numbers, the Union army was not going to last long. Someone needed to explain what had happened, so Garfield was summoned to Washington.

He felt that his principal purpose in going to the nation's capital was to defend Rosecrans's reputation before their superiors. But Garfield's conscience was also bothering him. He had been elected to Congress. The new Congress would meet in December. It was now late September. What should he do? Garfield discussed his future with Rosecrans, who strongly recommended he take his congressional seat. Still, Garfield was undecided.

"I will lay it before him [Mr. Lincoln] when I reach Washington, and let his decision settle the matter," Garfield said to Rosecrans.

In the District of Columbia, James called on the War Department. Located about a block west of the White House, it was a four-story affair, where telegraph lines snaked throughout, carrying messages to and from the battlefield commanders to the generals and others in Washington. Garfield was taken to a meeting, where he met Lincoln and Secretary Stanton.

He sat down to business. As the president and secretary of war watched, Garfield spread his maps out neatly on the table, explaining the military campaign he had just been a part of, doing everything he could to make Rosecrans look good. It didn't work.

It was clear who had done the heroic thing and who had not, thus saving the Army of the Potomac from annihilation. No one was more impressed than the president of the United States.

"I have never understood so fully and clearly the necessities, situation, and movements of any army in the field," said Lincoln. Whereupon he promptly promoted Garfield to major general, firing Rosecrans.

Garfield then spoke privately to the president, telling him of his quandary, which had just gotten worse. He had been given a promotion to major general, with all the responsibility that came with it. How could he leave and serve in Congress? Garfield happened to be asking the right president that question. In fact, each had once been in the same situation in combat, of having to challenge authority in order to be humane.[1]

During the Black Hawk War of 1832, Lincoln had been a captain. While he never saw combat, he did see "the corpse-strewn battlefields at Stillman's Run and Kellogg's Grove." That is how he learned what war was. Then, an Indian had wandered by the Kentuckians' encampment. Lincoln's men figured him for a spy and hustled him before a firing squad.

"Stop," Lincoln ordered.

The future sixteenth president made it clear to his men that if they wanted to murder the terrified man, they would have to go through him. His men stood down.[2] From his own experience, he knew Garfield's value as a courageous general. In fact, he had many generals—though probably none as brave as James Garfield. But he also knew that a man of such moral and physical courage would be as invaluable a political ally as he could ever hope to have.

Garfield had already saved his army. Now he would help him save the Union. The president finally spoke: "The Republican majority in Congress is very small. It is often doubtful whether we can carry [out] the necessary war measures. And besides, we are greatly lacking in men of military experience in the House, to regulate legislation about the army. It is your duty, therefore, to enter Congress, at any rate for the present."

He could not say no to his commander in chief.

Garfield agreed to serve his president and country by accepting his congressional seat. He was also a very good businessman. In negotiating his discharge from the army, it was with the agreement that his rank would be restored, if his political career didn't work out and he desired to go back to the military. Garfield resigned from the army.

The following day, he entered the House of Representatives as the newest member of the Ohio delegation.[3]

Abraham Lincoln knew how common it was for families to lose kids. Childhood mortality in the United States was high. In Massachusetts alone it was 15 percent.[4]

Lincoln and his wife, Mary, had had a son Edward. He was all of four years old when he died in 1850. His brother Willie, born that year, had a little better luck. He lived until he was twelve, dying of a "fever" in 1862. That left their youngest, Tad, and Robert, their firstborn, who wanted to serve the Union.

Would Lincoln agree to sacrifice his first son on the altar, not of the biblical Abraham's God, but that of the Union? Lincoln would have allowed Robert to enlist. Except that both men had Mary Todd Lincoln to contend with.

"[Father], [o]ur son is *not* more dear to us than the sons of other people are to their mothers," she told her husband.[5] Lincoln knew that meant, "Just try to rip my baby away from me."

While Lincoln figured out his strategy, Robert, who turned twenty-one in 1864, decided to continue his postgraduate studies at Harvard Law School. During a school break, he was returning south to the White House. It was late at night, and he found himself on a train platform in Jersey City, New Jersey.

Robert's platform was crowded with tired, agitated passengers. As was the custom, they were buying their berths from the overworked conductor, who stood like a sleepy sentinel, at the entrance to the sleeping car. The platform "was about the height of the car floor, and there was of course a narrow space between the platform and the car body," Robert later remembered.

He stood on the perimeter of the crowd, near the train. As passengers moved in closer to the conductor, Robert was "pressed by it [the crowd] against the car body, while waiting [his] turn." As the train began to move, Robert was twisted off his feet and dangled for a moment between life and eternity. Dropping meant certain death under the train's wheels.

Suddenly, someone reached down as he fell and grabbed Robert's coat collar.

"I was vigorously seized and quickly pulled up and out to a secure footing on the platform."

Disbelieving his luck, he looked up to thank his rescuer. Robert instantly recognized him.

"Edwin Booth!" Robert exclaimed in surprise and joy. Robert profusely thanked the famous actor for saving his life. It turned out they were on the same train south. Booth had a traveling companion, John T. Ford, the owner of Ford's theater in the District. He had wavy dark hair and eyebrows, accompanied by long dark muttonchops.

Edwin Booth and his even more famous acting brother, John Wilkes, were friendly with Robert.

When Robert got to Washington, the Great Emancipator celebrated the occasion by becoming the Great Compromiser. He made two deals. The first was with his wife, Mary. He promised that their son Robert would never be placed in the path of destruction. The second was with Ulysses S. Grant. Lincoln wrote his general, requesting that he assign Robert to his staff.

Considering that the war was winding down, it was probably the safest place to be. In January 1865, Robert took his place as one of the junior officers on Grant's staff. For the first time, in what would become a lifelong pattern, young Robert Lincoln was about to become an observer and participant in American history.[6]

10

"Hands Up!"

February 11, 1865

Dr. D. Willard Bliss was getting more national coverage. The old gray lady, the *New York Times*, referred to him as "the eminent surgeon in charge of Armory-square [*sic*] Hospital."

When Senator Thomas Holiday Hicks of Maryland collapsed in his room at Washington's Metropolitan Hotel, the *Times* reported that he was left "with paralysis of the left side on Friday last, and is now entirely prostrated by it." Bliss was Hicks's regular doctor.

When he served as Maryland's governor, Hicks had kept the border state on the Union side. That was a key to the Union's survival. The previous year, Hicks had had to get his left leg amputated below the knee. Bliss had wielded the saw. Hicks persevered and was able to walk again with the use of an artificial leg. But now Bliss was being called upon for something much worse.[1]

Bliss alighted from his carriage in front of the Metropolitan Hotel, a block-long, multistory structure. Just years before, it had been just a series of Federal-style attached brownstones, but when people began moving into Washington for work, the structures were converted into a hotel called Brown's.

In 1850 the Brown family had "hired celebrated Philadelphia architect John Haviland, a major proponent of the Greek Revival style. He gave the place a neoclassical façade made of white marble, reportedly from the same quarry as had supplied the Capitol building." Haviland enlarged the place upward, to a full five stories.

The beautifully renovated building reopened as Brown's Marble Hotel in 1851. Fourteen years later, the Brown family sold it, and the new owners renamed it the Metropolitan. When D. W. Bliss saw that at the top of the building the word "Metropolitan" was spelled out in a sign made of all white, capital letters, he knew that only the best stayed there.[2]

Bliss was led inside to the well-appointed suite of rooms occupied by Maryland's senior senator. After examining him, Bliss came up with his diagnosis: "The Doctor has pronounced his case ramalesement, or softening of the brain, and has cautioned his attendants for some time not to leave him alone day or night, apprehending that at any time the disease might result in hemaplegia, and yesterday he was suddenly summoned to witness the realization of his fears. For the last two weeks, however, he [Hicks] has not been in the Senate Chamber, and has been constantly in the charge of his attendants."[3]

Ramalesement, or softening of the brain (from the French term, *ramollissement*, "softening" or "weakening"), was a nineteenth-century term for what would later be called a stroke, or a cerebral hemorrhage. Bliss thought the senator's paralysis was a result of his brain getting soft. In fact, Senator Hicks had suffered a stroke. Bliss did not know what to do, so he left him to die. Senator Hicks obliged and died the following day.

Reporters converged on the Metropolitan to get the story. They discovered that one of the doctors who had attended Lincoln had also attended Hicks. The story went national on the following day in the *New York Times*.

What both cases actually had in common was that Bliss did nothing.

March 4, 1865

When the hubbub involving Bliss had died down, John P. Hale was jettisoned as a senator by the Vermont Republican Party. Not knowing what to do next, the now former senator decided to attend Lincoln's second inauguration. He arrived at the event with his twenty-four-year-old daughter, Lucy, who had her handsome, mustachioed fiancé in tow.

Like most fathers, Hale dearly loved his daughter Lucy, who had dressed to the nines for Lincoln's inauguration on the Capital's steps. As he was sitting there, Hale became agitated about Lucy's choice in men. He had felt this way for awhile. He just didn't like her fiancé. Sure, he was famous, good-looking, and well heeled, but there was just something off about him that Hale couldn't put his finger on.

Hale was in the same position as many fathers whose daughters fall in love with men they do not approve of. Lucy was smitten. The charming and dashingly handsome love of Lucy's life wrote her a love letter for Valentine's Day: "You resemble in a most remarkable degree a lady, very dear to me, now dead and your close resemblance to her surprised me the first time I saw you. To see you has indeed offered me a melancholy pleasure."[4]

Perhaps Lucy Hale should have given more thought to a compliment comparing her appearance to a dead woman's. However, his words mesmerized her, as did her beau, who was now by her side. Also listening to Lincoln's second inauguration speech was Dr. Charles Leale, who had walked over from Armory Square Hospital, just a block down the Mall.

Leale observed the "almost divine appearance of the President's face in the glow of the light from the White House." He decided to study his face at his next public appearance.[5]

• • •

Robert E. Lee had to admit that it was over. Despite the best efforts of the brave men it was his honor to command, on April 3, the Confederate capital of Richmond fell to Union troops. Out fought, out flanked, ill provisioned, to continue fighting meant extinction. Grant had practically surrounded them. Four days later, the Union's commanding general, sat down in his tent at his writing desk, and wrote out this note.

5 P.M., April 7th, 1865

General R. E. Lee, Commanding, C.S.A.:

The results of the last week must convince you of the hopelessness of further resistance on the part of the Army of Northern Virginia in this struggle. I feel that it is so, and regard it as my duty to shift from myself the responsibility of any further effusion of blood, by asking of you the surrender of that portion of the Confederate States army known as the Army of Northern Virginia.

U.S. Grant, Lieutenant-General

A rider carried the message through Confederate lines. After he read it, Lee promptly responded:

April 7th, 1865

General: I have received your note of this date. Though not entertaining the opinion you express of the hopelessness of further resistance on the part of the Army of Northern Virginia, I reciprocate your desire to avoid useless effusion of blood, and therefore, before considering your proposition, ask the terms you will offer on condition of its surrender.[6]

Lee's message to Grant was not received until after midnight of the next day. By then, George Armstrong Custer had handed Grant his ace in the hole.

April 8, 1865

"Hands up!" Fred Blodgett shouted, leveling the barrel of his rifle at the train engineer's heart.

Brevet Major General George Armstrong Custer had seen a lot of action since Bull Run and received many promotions. Between that big iron on his hip and his battle charges, he had blazed his way into the history books as the youngest general in United States history, and was nicknamed the Boy General.

The twenty-six-year-old commanded his own division, which he had marched to the town of Appomattox Station, in northern Virginia. His spies told him that four supply trains were about to arrive simultaneously. Custer decided to stop them from distributing their much-needed supplies. Fred Blodgett was with the Second New York Cavalry, under Custer's command.

Blodgett rode up to the first train engine he saw and leveled his carbine at the train's engineer, who peered down from the cab.

"Hands up!" Blodgett shouted.

Before the cavalrymen could consolidate their plans, the Confederate artillery opened up on them. It was about 4:00 p.m. Custer's men fought for some three hours, until dusk, charging the enemy in short bursts. They finally beat the Confederates back, across the Richmond-Lynchburg Stage Road. By commandeering the Stage Road, Grant's army had now cut off Lee's line of retreat.[7]

After reading Lee's note regarding terms of surrender, Grant took quill in hand and wrote:

April 8th, 1865

General R. E. Lee, Commanding C.S.A.:

Your note of last evening in reply to mine of the same date, asking the conditions on which I will accept the surrender of the Army of Northern Virginia, is just received. In reply I would say that, peace being my great desire, there is but one condition I would insist upon, namely, that the men and officers surrendered shall be disqualified for taking up arms against the Government of the United States until properly exchanged.

I will meet you, or will designate officers to meet any officers you may name for the same purpose, at any point agreeable to you, for the purpose of arranging definitely the terms upon which the surrender of the Army of Northern Virginia will be received.

U.S. Grant, Lieutenant-General[8]

The two generals exchanged notes for the next two days, until they agreed to meet in the village of Appomattox Courthouse, at Wilmer McLean's home at the crossroads. Arriving alone, Lee was first for a change. He sat down by himself in the large, fancy first-floor sitting room. A few minutes later, Grant walked in. He, too, was alone.

Grant had left his staff to cool their spurs outside. He wanted to speak to Lee alone. About five minutes later, Grant opened the door and invited his staff in. Among them were Lt. Robert Lincoln and Gen. Horace Porter.

"We walked in softly and found General Grant sitting at a marble-topped table, in the center of the room. Lee [was] sitting beside a small oval table near the front window, in the corner opposite the door by which we entered, and facing General Grant. We ranged ourselves quietly about the sides of the room, very much as people enter a sick-chamber when they expect to find the patient dangerously," Porter later remembered.[9]

Dressed in his crisp new uniform, Robert Lincoln watched as the two generals signed the terms of surrender. Lee soon went on his way. As he rode out, Grant and all the Union officers raised their hats in deference. Robert put his hat back on his head and went to the White House to see his parents.

April 14, 1865, Morning, Good Friday

It was a pretty good breakfast. On this morning, Abraham Lincoln had his whole family around the White House breakfast table.[10]

Directly across from him sat his wife, Mary, whom he called "Mother." On the left was eldest son, Robert, in full dress uniform. Across from Robert sat his twelve-year-old kid brother, Tad. While eating, Robert showed his father a picture of Robert E. Lee. Lincoln studied it carefully.

"It is a good face. It is the face of a noble, noble, brave man. I am glad the war is over at last," he said.

Like any father would when given the opportunity to address his adult child of his concerns, Lincoln turned to Robert.

"Well, my son, you have returned safely from the front. The war is now closed, and we soon will live in peace, with the brave men that have been fighting against us. I trust that the era of good feeling has returned, and henceforth we shall live in peace. Now listen to me, Robert. You must lay aside your uniform, and return to college. I wish you to read law for three years, and at the end of that time, I hope that we will be able to tell whether you will make a lawyer or not."[11]

While showing concern, his father was also showing his doubts about his oldest son. Mary Lincoln decided to change the subject.

"I have tickets to Grover's Theatre, but I'd prefer to see *Our American Cousin* at Ford's Theatre," she said.

Even the First Lady couldn't get a ticket to the latter, so they were going to the former. Mary had invited Robert to accompany them. Weary from his journey from Appomattox, Robert begged off and decided to stay at the White House that night.

Later that day, Dr. Charles Leale heard that President and Mrs. Lincoln had instead changed their minds, or Mary had, and were going to attend *Our American Cousin* at Ford's Theatre. Leale figured that after finishing his duties at Armory Square, he'd change quickly and rush to the theater. He wanted to study the president's face and expressions.[12]

But before going to the theater, Lincoln had business to do. He met with John P. Hale. The guy needed a break. Supporting Dr. D. W. Bliss had cost him his senate seat and his political career. Lincoln came to his rescue and appointed his fellow Republican the United States ambassador to Spain. For his part, Hale hoped that his daughter Lucy would accompany him to Spain, leaving her beloved behind.

It is not unlikely that, as one father to another, Hale told Lincoln about his anxieties over her daughter's fiancé. His name was John Wilkes Booth. Unknown to both of them, Booth was a secret Confederate agent.

1. President James Garfield.
Photograph courtesy of the Library
of Congress LC-USZ62-209.

2. Dr. D. Willard Bliss. Photograph courtesy of the U.S. National Park Service.

3. (*Opposite top*) A portrait of the entire Garfield clan. Photograph courtesy of the Library of Congress LC-DIG-pga-05865.

4. (*Opposite bottom*) Alexander Graham and Mabel Bell in a humorous pose, during one of Bell's flight experiments. Photograph courtesy of the Gilbert H. Grosvenor Collection of Photographs of the Alexander Graham Bell Family, Library of Congress LC-DIG-ds-06862.

5. (*Opposite top*) Lucretia Garfield as a middle-aged woman. Photograph courtesy of the Brady-Handy Collection, Library of Congress LC-USZ62-25793.

6. (*Opposite bottom*) John Wilkes Booth, the matinee idol and presidential assassin. Photograph courtesy of the Library of Congress LC-DIG-npcc-19612.

7. (*Above*) The cover of *Puck*, a humor magazine, depicting the absurdity of the trial of Charles Guiteau. Illustration courtesy of the Library of Congress LC-USZC4-6402.

8. The place on the Chickamauga Battlefield where the Widow Glenn's cabin stood. Photograph courtesy of the author.

9. George Armstrong Custer, the Boy General, during the Civil War. Photograph courtesy of the Hoxie Collection, Library of Congress LC-DIG-ppmsca-33129.

10. Alexander Graham Bell as an
older man. Photograph courtesy
of the Library of Congress
LC-USZ62-14759.

11. William Howard Taft, Warren
G. Harding, and Robert Lincoln
at the inauguration of his father's
monument in 1922. Photograph
courtesy of the Library of
Congress LC-DIG-npcc-06391.

PART TWO

Fast is fine but accuracy
is everything.

—Wyatt Earp

"God Reigns, and the Government at Washington Still Lives!"

April 14, 1865, Evening, Good Friday

"Everything that bore his name was given up, even the little picture of himself, hung over my babies' beds in the nursery," Asia Booth later wrote. "He had placed it there himself saying, 'Remember me, babies, in your prayers.'"

"Wilkes" as his sister Asia called him, had "long, up-curling [eye]lashes, perfectly shaped hands, [his] father's finely shaped head [and his mother's] black hair and large hazel eyes."

To America, John Wilkes Booth was the handsome matinee idol who made women swoon and men jealous. But beneath the handsome façade and intelligent mind was a delusion—Lincoln was about to establish a monarchy.[1]

John T. Ford was in Richmond, Virginia. But it made no difference. Booth's presence at his theater was common. Booth liked to be around the place when he wasn't performing there. His entry to the theater before the crowds arrived, without a ticket, was of no interest, nor was the horse waiting for Booth, in the alley behind the theater.

Suddenly in mid-play, the stage door burst open. Booth limped out, his face contorted in pain. He limped as quickly as he could to the horse, then pulled himself painfully up into the saddle. Inside his shiny boot, his ankle was already swelling up, as the broken ankle bone pushed against his skin, straining to break it.

In intense pain, he thrust the damaged limb into the stirrup. Asia knew him as a "fearless" rider. Booth showed it. Ignoring the searing pain, he put his steel spurs to his horse's flanks, galloped down the alley, out into the open street.

Behind him, Booth heard the screams as the doors of Ford's Theatre burst open. Theatergoers, who moments before were laughing at a play, were now screaming in panic.

"The president's been shot."

"He's dead!"

"Someone call the police."

"What happened?"

What had happened was that earlier in the day, Lincoln had invited Grant, as well as his victorious commander's wife, to accompany him and his wife to the theater. It was a great honor to be invited, but the Grants turned the president down. The war was over, so for Grant, business came first, and they had a business engagement in Philadelphia.

The president's staff eventually recruited Clara Harris, a twenty-year-old New York City socialite, and her twenty-year-old fiancé, Major Henry Reed Rathbone. They would be Lincoln and Mary's company that night in the president's box.

Dr. Charles Leale had bought a seat for seventy-five cents in the dress circle, forty feet below the presidential box.[2] The play had started when the group of four entered the theater. Leale watched as actors stopped performing and the orchestra struck up "Hail to the Chief." Acknowledging a thunderous ovation, the presidential party paused several times.

Leale deeply admired the etched lines in Lincoln's face, looking like something you would see on a piece of classical Greek statuary. As the play started again, everyone's attention turned toward the stage.

Well, not everyone's attention.

Somewhere in the scaffolding of the theater, Booth knew it was almost time for the performance of his career. Dressed in black for the occasion, sporting that pair of shiny steel spurs, the actor moved like a phantom, unseen, above the theatergoers below. When he got to the presidential box, he saw that it was unguarded. Booth had cased it prior to the performance.

Silently, Booth opened the door of the box. His target was sitting in a tall, straight-backed chair, with his back to him, watching the play unfold on stage. The other three people in the box with the president were doing the same thing. Listening to the dialogue, Booth waited as planned, until Harry Hawk, an actor he despised as being too melodramatic, was about to say a line in the play that draws a big laugh. Booth knew that line; the audience would erupt in laughter.

That would, he believed, stifle the sound of the shot from his powerful .44-caliber eight-ounce derringer, with a two-and-a-half-inch barrel.[3] Taking the derringer out of his pocket, he held it in a steady hand. Booth lined up his target through the gun's sight.

He had waited for this moment for a long time. Booth was going to stop the Lincoln monarchy. As Hawk said the line, the audience laughed as one and Booth fired. The bullet hit Lincoln in the back of the head, on the left side, and embedded deep in his brain.

As he slumped over in his chair, Mary rushed over to support his head. Major Rathbone who sat on the other side of the box, instantly recognized Booth, who quickly dropped the one-shot derringer and pulled a horn-handled dagger from his waistband.

Moving with a fencer's agility, Rathbone was on his feet and across the box. Before Booth escaped, Rathbone was going to tackle him. The blade flashed and Booth brought it down, slashing Rathbone's left arm, opening it from shoulder to elbow. But that didn't stop this battle-tested soldier. Rathbone lunged for Booth yet a second time.

Booth evaded the weakened man easily. That's when Clara Harris came to life.

"The president is shot!" she screamed.

Like some Dickensian hero escaping his past, Booth was on the edge of the box, ready to leap to the stage.

"Stop that man!" Rathbone yelled, cradling his bloodied arm.[4]

Through his opera glasses, Leale looked up and saw Booth's flashing dark eyes. Leale watched him push off into space and hang suspended for a moment. As he dropped, one of his steel spurs hooked the flag that fluttered from the presidential box, turning his ankle.

It caused Booth to land badly, his ankle cracking as he landed. But Booth was a trooper. Knowing this was his farewell performance, he raised himself to his feet and turned triumphantly to the audience that had always loved him.

"*Sic semper tyrannis*. The South is avenged! I have done it!" he yelled in lunatic triumph.

By then, Charles Leale was on his feet and running.

"Kill the murderer!" somebody shouted near him.

"Shoot him, shoot him," others yelled in the theater.

Leale ran up the stairs and when he entered the box, he saw Lincoln still seated in a high backed armchair, his head leaning toward his right side, supported by Mrs. Lincoln, who was weeping inconsolably. Clara Harris was on Mary's left, behind the president.

"I am a United States surgeon," Leale announced.

Mary Lincoln looked at the young man with the receding hairline and the close-set dark eyes. He combed his coal-black hair to the right side of his head, to hide the encroaching baldness. Long sideburns snaked down his cheeks, sharp nose presiding over a drooping mustache.

"Oh, Doctor, do what you can for him, do what you can!" cried Mary Lincoln, getting the words out in a stifling sob.

"I will do everything I can."

"Oh, Doctor! Is he dead? Can he recover? Will you take charge of him? Do what you can for him. Oh, my dear husband!" Mary wailed.[5]

Before he could act, Rathbone came up to Leale.

"Please attend to my wound," the major asked weakly.

Leale placed his hand under Rathbone's chin and looked him in the eyes. Seeing he was in no mortal danger, Leale attended to the president first. People were already crowding into the box. Leale sent one man for brandy and another for water. Then he looked down at his patient. Slumped in the chair, Lincoln's eyes were closed. Leale put his fingers on his radial pulse; there was none.

Having recently graduated from medical college, Leale had had his baptism under fire at Armory Square, with its tremendous mortality rate. He wasn't one to give up. Trying to figure out a way to revive him, Leale had some men help place Lincoln on the floor of the box. Remembering that Booth had had a dagger, Leale thought Lincoln might have been stabbed.

"Cut his coat and shirt open from the neck to the elbow," he directed a man.

Leale wanted to check the hemorrhage that he thought might have taken place from the subclavian artery or another blood vessel. While kneeling on the floor over his head, with his eyes continuously watching the president's face, he watched as the work was done with a dirk knife. But no wound was found there.

Leale then lifted his eyelids and saw "evidence of a brain injury." Feeling around for the bullet wound, he finally discovered it in the back of the president's head. He inserted his finger, hopeful it had not gone in too deep for removal. Discovering it had, he removed a clot of blood at the entrance, which reduced the pressure on Lincoln's brain, but he was still not breathing.

Leale wouldn't give up.

It was time to try artificial respiration.

Leale knelt on the wooden floor over the president, with a knee on each side of his pelvis, facing him. Leaning forward, he opened his mouth and inserted two extended fingers of his right hand and pressed the base of his paralyzed tongue downward and outward. That opened his larynx and made a free passage for air to enter the lungs.

Just then, two doctors, Taft and King, who had been in the audience below, arrived to help. Leale placed Taft at one of Lincoln's arms and King at the other to manipulate them in order to expand his thorax, then slowly to press the arms down by the side of the body, while he pressed the diaphragm upward. This forced air to be drawn in and out of Lincoln's lungs.

With the thumb and fingers of his right hand, Leale used sliding pressure beneath Lincoln's ribs, to stimulate his heart. It worked. Leale heard a feeble heartbeat and irregular breathing. He had brought the president back from death. Almost in celebration, the brandy and water then arrived.

Leale put a little of it into Lincoln's immobile mouth. Some of it dribbled down into his whiskers, but most of it found its way into his throat. After consulting with Taft and King, Leale decided to have the president moved to the nearest house for whatever further treatment they could offer. On the basis of what he observed, Leale wasn't holding out much hope, but he was determined to try.

When they tried to leave the presidential box, they encountered a huge, curious, and concerned crowd blocking their way.

"Guards, clear the passage!" Leale shouted.

Union army soldiers, who weeks before had been fighting Southerners, now held back their own as Lincoln was carried by the three doctors and two others, over their heads, blood dripping as they exited the box and went down the stairs. The crowd got as silent as it had been noisy and watched with grief and fear. The five men, bearing the nation's heavy burden, carried Lincoln out the theater's front doors.

Making sure they didn't slip on horse dung, the men quickly crossed the muddy street. Looking for a place to take the wounded and dying president, they didn't know where to go. People from nearby houses had crowded into the street, wondering what would happen next. The five men stopped in the middle of the street, looking around desperately for refuge.

A man appeared with a lamp in front of Petersen's Boarding House, directly across from the theater.

"Bring him in here!" he shouted, gesturing.

The men carried Lincoln into the parlor of Petersen's.

"Up the stairs," the man ordered.

They carried Lincoln up a narrow set of stairs and threw open the door of a room. The room was small, with slatted chairs and cane seats scattered about, and a rocking chair of the same type Lincoln had favored in the White House. The walls were decorated with patterned gray wallpaper, broken up with vertical tan strips sporting a fleur-de-lis design.

"GOD REIGNS, WASHINGTON STILL LIVES!"

There was a small table with a pitcher of water and a basin, both of which were white with a Chinese design of blue patterned across them. There was a nightstand on the far wall, with a black hairbrush and black comb, and a small, shiny metal box that belonged to the absent occupant. Next to the nightstand was a bed, on which they placed the wounded man.

But Lincoln's legs were much too long for it.

"Let's place him diagonally," said Leale, and the men followed his instructions.

But the bed was still too short.

"Let's move the foot of the bed," Leale requested. "That will enable us to place him in a comfortable position."

The room had already filled with anxious people, some of whom removed the wooden foot of the bed so the president's feet could dangle over comfortably.

"Captain," Leale called.

When the officer entered the room, Leale asked him to open a window.

"I'd like everyone but the surgeons to leave the room," he then announced.

He needed privacy to do a more thorough examination of the president. Everyone began to leave, except for Mary Lincoln; she was staying.

"Surgeon," said the captain. "Your order has been carried out, except for Mrs. Lincoln. I do not like speaking to her."

Leale turned and strode over to the First Lady.

"Mrs. Lincoln, would you please leave, so I can examine your husband further?" he asked.

Without further protest, Mary Todd Lincoln took her leave. Once she left, Leale examined the president's entire body from head to foot. Finding no other injury, Leale removed his clothes and covered him with blankets, because his legs and feet were ice cold.

"Get some hot water and more blankets," Leale ordered.

The men did as they were told and the items soon appeared. Leale applied the blankets to his abdomen, legs, and feet in an effort to try and raise Lincoln's body temperature, but Leale knew it was to no avail.

"His wound is mortal. It is impossible for him to recover."

His words were passed to Mary Lincoln, who broke down in utter grief.

An officer approached Leale.

"What can I do for you, Surgeon?"

Leale thought for a few moments.

"Please send messengers to the White House for the President's son, Captain Robert T. Lincoln. Also contact the Surgeon General, Joseph K. Barnes, surgeon D. Willard Bliss, in charge of Armory Square General Hospital, the president's family physician, Dr. Robert K. Stone, and each member of the president's cabinet."

Robert was at the White House when he got Leale's summons. He had spent the evening with John Hay, his friend who was also one of Lincoln's two private secretaries. When he got the message that his father had been shot, he rushed outside to a waiting hansom that whisked him away to the Petersen House.[6]

No sooner had he gotten there than the three physicians also arrived. Barnes's "personal appearance was striking—tall, well proportioned, and commanding in figure, while his face possessed elements of strength, which were apparent even to the casual observer."[7]

Leale assigned Barnes and Stone tasks to assist him in treating the president. Despite the fact that Bliss was his boss, Leale gave him nothing to do, even when his specialty came up. By then it was 2:00 a.m. Leale sent for a Nelaton probe. When it arrived, Leale entrusted Surgeon General Barnes with the task of inserting it about two-and-a-half inches into Lincoln's head. Bliss was forced to watch as the probe "came in contact with a foreign substance, which lay across the track of the ball."

Barnes kept going until the probe was inserted several inches further, when it again touched a hard substance. But when the porcelain bulb of the probe was extracted, it had not turned green, the unmistakable mark of lead. The probe was then inserted a second time by Barnes. After withdrawing it, he conferred with Barnes's assistant, Major Charles Henry Crane, and Robert Stone.[8]

The three agreed they had found the ball. As Leale thought, death was imminent. As for Bliss, he was forced to watch as history unfolded without him. Leale never consulted with him for anything.

April 15, 1865, Holy Saturday

It had been hours of agony waiting for his father to die.

For much of that time, while the doctors administered to him, Robert was out of the room. Gideon Welles, who was also present, later observed that on the occasions when Robert was there, he "bore himself well, but two [times] gave way to overpowering grief and sobbed aloud, turning his head and leaning on the shoulder of Senator Sumner."[9]

Surgeon General Barnes held his finger to Lincoln's carotid artery, while Major Crane held his head. Dr. Stone, who was sitting on the bed, held his left pulse. Leale held his right. When Leale could no longer feel it, and he was sure Abraham Lincoln was dead, he looked at his watch.

"It is 7:22 a.m.," he said, pronouncing the time of death of the first U.S president to be assassinated.

• • •

James Garfield happened to be visiting New York City, when he received word of the president's assassination. He liked the city. The day after Lincoln's murder, he spoke extemporaneously to a mob of panicked New Yorkers, who were fearful the nation would not survive the president's assassination: "Fellow citizens, clouds and darkness are round about Him. His pavilion is dark waters and thick clouds of the skies. Justice and judgment are the establishment of His throne! Mercy and truth shall go before His face! Fellow citizens, God reigns, and the Government at Washington still lives!"

Thanks to the *New York Times*, the *New York World*, the *Herald*

Tribune, and all the other New York City papers whose reporting went around the country over the telegraph wires this last sentence became known throughout the United States. The following year, on the first anniversary of Lincoln's assassination, Garfield rose on the floor of Congress to address his colleagues: "It was no one man who killed Abraham Lincoln; it was the embodied spirit of treason and slavery, inspired with fearful and despairing hate, that struck him down, in the moment of the nation's supremest joy."[10]

James Garfield always did have a way with words. Putting his gun and saber down was much easier than he had anticipated, but he was not trained as a soldier. George Armstrong Custer was.

With the war over, Custer's wartime brevet rank of brigadier general reverted to that of lieutenant colonel of his new command, the Seventh Cavalry. He and Alexander Graham Bell would subsequently find fame on the same day.

12

"You Don't Really Feel You Are Going
into the Backwoods, Do You?"

While Robert, Mary, and Tad Lincoln were feeling grief over their loss in Washington, across the Atlantic in London, Melville Sr., Eliza, Alec, Melly, and Ted Bell, were grieving over theirs. Melville Bell also had a way with words. He had been putting the finishing touches on his Visible Speech system, when his father died. Alec Bell stood with Melville and the rest of his family, at the gravesite of Grandfather Bell at Highgate Cemetery, in the northern part of the city, as he was lowered into his grave.

Looking around him, Alec saw Gothic tombs and rows of tombstones, surrounded by copses of trees. And since the place was only twenty-nine years old, even the stones didn't look that weathered. Surrounding them was as a "romantic profusion of trees, memorials and wildlife," meant to help the mourners manage their grief. Even here, at life's end, was a place bursting with life.[1]

His grandfather's death triggered a big change in young Alec's life; his father decided to move the family to London. Despite this upheaval, Alec worked doggedly on his experiments with sound. He decided he needed a real subject and enlisted Trouve, the family's Skye terrier.

Bell would push his supple hands into the dog's mouth and manipulate Trouve's lips to form what sounded like words. He knew this was nothing more than a parlor trick. How to apply it to actual human speech was the real test. The question that buzzed through Bell's mind was how to transmit sound clearly.

Samuel Morse had already invented the telegraph, but that only transmitted "clicks and clacks," in a system of dots and dashes that had to be translated by the receiving telegrapher into words.

Written words. What about real sound? How can I get it to go from here to there? Bell wondered.

Bell began to experiment with tuning forks. He formed a device with which he was able to change their resonance. But he was having trouble and got increasingly frustrated.

"Write Ellis and see what he thinks," his father suggested.

Bell composed a letter to his father's friend, philologist Alexander Ellis, telling him of his interest in transmitting sound and asking for educational resources. Ellis, who himself would become famous years later as Shaw's model for Professor Henry Higgins in *Pygmalion*, replied:

Dear Alec,

I hope this letter finds you and your family well. You may be interested in knowing that your experiments with sound are similar to the ones currently underway in Germany. Here's a book that may help you.

Sincerely, Alexander Ellis

He enclosed a copy of *On the Sensations of Tone as a Physiological Basis for the Theory of Music* by Hermann von Helmholtz. In it, von Helmholtz wrote about his experiments to convey the sound of vowels through a series of tuning forks that he had set up in his laboratory. Once again, Bell translated a German book into English.

This time, Bell's knowledge of German was not up to par. He misinterpreted some of the text. Bell thought von Helmholtz had actually produced articulate speech through his tuning fork contraption. No matter how hard he tried adapting his own tuning fork apparatus to what the German had made, he could not replicate articulate speech.

It was a fortuitous mistake. When he eventually realized that the German had not done this, he came upon the idea that would make history.

"I came to believe firmly in the feasibility of the telegraphic transmission of speech," Bell later wrote.

Besides his experiments, Bell began assisting his father with Visible Speech lectures and demonstrations at a private school for the deaf in South Kensington. But while teaching, Bell began to experience headaches and sleeplessness. It was something the eighteen-year-old would suffer from for the rest of his life. And he wasn't the only Bell son with health problems.

Younger brother Edward, whom the family called "Ted," began coughing. Melville and Eliza hoped against hope that it wasn't consumption, the dreaded wasting disease that seemed to literally consume the victim. "So long as [he] keeps still, he is not much troubled with his cough," Eliza wrote to Alec Bell who was then teaching in Bath.

Eliza's optimism was understandable. What mother wants to bury a son?

Within months, Ted was discovered to have consumption. Coughing constantly, Ted began to lose weight quickly, his cheeks sinking back into his head, the sallow skin turning yellow, pulled taught against his skull. And then, Ted died.

"Sorrow we can never cease to feel for the loss of our darling Edward. He was a dear, good boy and our way will be dark without him," his mother wrote again to Alec.

Helping the Bells to emerge from their grief over Ted's untimely death was Melly. Following in his father's footsteps, he had established his own elocution school where he, too, taught Visible Speech. And he fell in love with a girl, Carrie Ottoway, who loved him. They were going to marry. Melly was giving his parents what the Cockney Jews called in Yiddish *naches*. It means great pleasure

Alec, though, was not as lucky in romance. Melly's successes just seemed to reflect Alec's failures with women.

"I only wish I was as fortunate as Melly is," he wrote to his parents.

Earlier in his life, Melville Sr. had himself recovered from a debilitating illness only through a lengthy period of salubrious recovery in Canada. While he'd moved the family to London for economic opportunity, the family finances were not improving. Furthermore, it was thought that the smoky air of cities fed the spread of consumption.

Maybe that was why after his youngest son's death, he traveled to America to promote Visible Speech. Maybe it was a better place to live, with more opportunity. In Boston, Melville Bell met lawyer Gardner Greene Hubbard, who knew of Melville's reputation. The wealthy businessman had financed a school for the deaf, at which his daughter, Mabel, was a pupil.

Traveling on to Toronto, Melville Sr. chatted up old acquaintances. Then when he got home, Melville began to think like an immigrant—someone who was willing to leave his home country to go to another, in order to provide his family with a better life. He thought clearly about moving his family across the ocean to America, a place that, if on his just completed trip, the acceptance of his Visible Speech system was any indication, it was a place that offered prosperity.

But in 1870, as Melville's plans to relocate the family came closer to fruition, tragedy struck the Bell family yet again. Melly was stricken with consumption. Powerless to act, Alec watched as his brother lay in his hospital bed, getting weaker and weaker, until he, too, wasted away. Particularly close to Melly, Alec was devastated by his death.

He took solace in his teaching and the prospect of marriage. He asked a woman he had been courting, Marie Eccleston, for her hand in marriage; she rejected him. But his teaching career was expanding. The government was considering putting government money into deaf education. And then there was another girl he liked, Maggie Herdman, his old friend Ben's sister.

And there were his experiments with sound and teaching. The last thing on Bell's mind was immigrating. But there was an urgency in Melville and Eliza's pleas to move with them. He was their only surviving son. That left him with a responsibility to . . . survive. So he agreed to immigrate with them.

Alec Bell helped his parents sell almost everything—Melly's property, their property, and most of their possessions.

"I collected all the things that were to be kept into the study—and locked myself in—and tried to imagine myself in the Backwoods of Canada. It was not very hard to imagine . . . sitting on chairs—in [my] empty classroom," Bell wrote his mother.

Considering his towering intellect, it is highly doubtful that Bell thought that all of Canada was "backwoods." He was just mourning what he had lost and what he thought he was leaving behind. Eliza wrote him back with parental understanding: "You don't really think you are going into the back-woods, do you? You are merely going into a country house, and will have civilized society there, just as much as you have here."

Thinking over his mother's words carefully must have been a great source of inspiration to him. And so young Bell walked up the gangplank onto the ss *Nestorian*, the ship that would take him and his family to Canada.

Like so many immigrants before and since, the Melville Bell family braved the seven-day Atlantic crossing, searching for a new, healthy, and prosperous life for themselves on the other side of the ocean, on the North American continent. While Melville was making plans for his twenty-three-year-old son's future, Alec was making his on the *Nestorian*'s deck.

Over those seven days, the Atlantic's waves were as smooth as Delphine glass, when it was fine for him to promenade the deck's shiny planks and smoke his pipe. The sun beat down like rays of light coming from heaven. But then, when they hit bad weather, the sky darkened and the Atlantic swelled up to four stories.

The *Nestorian* bounced back and forth over the waves. Alec's stomach was like the waves; and as he wrestled with his stomach, he naturally thought of his own mortality, because if the ship leaned over too far, it wasn't coming back. Alec thought about what this new life he was sailing toward really meant to his future.

"A man's own judgment should be the final appeal in all that relates to himself," he wrote in his Thought Book, a small notebook he carried with him everywhere.

Bell resolved to be what a later generation would call his "own man." This was not going to be easy. First and foremost he was his father's son, a speech teacher. And yet, there was something else driving him, an inner belief that he could make a difference in people's lives with something that he made.

The family disembarked in the old Canadian seaport of Nova Scotia. Their hansom cab took them over cobblestone streets to the railroad station, where the Bell family embarked on a train ride west, to Brantford, a small Western Ontario town. The Bell family once again set down roots, this time on a ten-and-a-half-acre farm. Alec began to construct a laboratory, from which to study the human voice and continue his experiments.

And his father, Melville? His fame had preceded him. He began to lecture throughout the Canadian provinces, making good money to boot. Executing his plan for Alec, he got him jobs lecturing on his Visible Speech system, in Boston and New England. The next thing Alec knew, he was on a train going south across the border.[2]

He went through the United States for the first time, marveling at the vastness of its forests, the limestone formations in Vermont, the industriousness of the inhabitants who had carved out farms in the most unlikely of places. When he finally arrived in Boston, it was to a scene of vast activity, much like London.

Boston seemed to have a life of its own, an energy that permeated up from the harbor stocked with steamships and schooners; and smells, oh those smells, of fresh-baked bread and something Italian in the city's West End, right up through the downtown area stocked with brick and mortar buildings, multistory structures that seemed to climb toward the clear blue sky.

For the next two years, Alec Bell taught Visible Speech at schools for the deaf in Boston. But he was torn. There were only so many hours in a day. Could he best put his energies into teaching speech with his father's system or as an inventor?

13

"The Doctor Declares that the Minister Does Not Own an Acre of Land There"

The popular myth won out. Everyone believed that Dr. D. W. Bliss had treated Abraham Lincoln. For Bliss, it was a lesson well learned. His practice in Washington DC's Fourth Ward thrived, exactly because of the acceptance of this lie, which he never corrected. That just encouraged Bliss's next "venture."

From out of Ecuador in South America came word that a cure for cancer had been found. The medical community in the District of Columbia, as well as the United States, looked at cancer as an untreatable, incurable disease.

If this "cure," were true, it would change history. What was it? It was cundurango, the bark of a South American tree. Bliss jumped on the cundurango bandwagon. He wanted to make money. So he began to market cundurango as a cancer cure, despite the fact that there was nothing to prove it worked.

Bliss promoted this cure in person with the patients in his practice and in newspaper advertisements that he took out, where he sold the bark. He became so well known for his "cundurango cure," that for the second time, he made the pages of the *New York Times.*

CUNDURANGO

The latest Report from Dr. Bliss—When a Supply may be Expected—

Its Wonderful Virtues

The victims of cancer who have been anxiously looking forward to a time not far distant when they would be able to procure a sup-ply [*sic*] of the South American specific "cundurango," will be pleased to learn that Dr. D. W. Bliss of Washington expects very soon to obtain a sufficient quantity to furnish all who may be in need of it.

Bliss told the *Times* that a naval officer based in New York had asked for some of the wonder specific (cure) for a friend. Bliss explained he had none to spare, yet. "I receive but a small quantity at a time, and it being my purpose to treat a few cases here, where they can be under my own observation, it will be impossible for me to send any of it away. The remedy, as well as myself having been attacked, I desire to demonstrate to the public what it will do, which necessitates the above course."

Bliss claimed that the Washington DC medical society's antagonism toward him was because they wanted to stifle his cancer cure. For the few that knew about it, that brought to mind the failed inventions Bliss had gotten Lincoln to pay for. He then made the even more outrageous charge that the Washington medical society was under the spell of former Confederates.

The charges Bliss was bringing were about as broad as the gap in the line Rosecrans created at Chickamauga. Bliss went on to tell the *Times* that he expected a "sufficient quantity" of cundurango by August 15 "to supply the profession or the public as they desire." He claimed, "From the statements of the physicians of Quito [Ecuador] and my own experience in its use, I am convinced that the 'cundurango' is quite as reliable as a specific [cure] in cancer.[1]

As Bliss continued to push his "cundurango cure," the medical community finally reacted, expelling him from the Medical Association of the District of Columbia. On July 13, 1871, the *Michigan Democrat* reported:

> There were several serious charges against him [said the report issued by the Medical Association of the District of Columbia] one of which was quackery in trying to force a medicine upon the country, which he knew had not the virtue claimed for it. The Association took up another charge, that of consulting in the case of Vice President Colfax, with Dr. C. C. Cox, who had been previously refused admission

"THE DOCTOR DECLARES"

into said Association, on account of his holding a seat in the Board of Health with Dr. Verdi, a homeopathic physician, and for this expelled him.

Concerning Cundurango, which has excited the attention of the medical profession throughout the country, a learned physician says, 'It is our belief that no medicine will ever be found to cure schirrus, or cancer. It is impossible that this should be so from the very nature of the case. The malignant cell growth which constitutes schirrus, or cancer, is a hereditary disease, depending upon the physical constitution of the individual.

What tuberculous deposits is to the brain and bone in children, and to the lungs and intestines in adults, cancerous degeneration is to men and women of mature age. It can only be cured by a power that can remove its cause—i.e., that can change the whole texture of the organism. Cundurango can never do this.

Never one to go through channels especially when his reputation was at stake, Bliss had gone even further, as the *Democrat* continued in its report the next day.

Dr. Bliss met in consultation with another physician of Washington not of the 'regular' school, but who holds a position upon the Board of Health with a homeopathic practitioner. But the real reason of the expulsion is political, and springs from the ex-rebel element which practically rules in that medical society.

The paper then compared Bliss to Lincoln.

Dr. Bliss has been an ardent advocate of recognizing real merit wherever found, and therefore of admitting well-qualified *colored* physicians into the association. He is not a mealy-mouthed nor timid man, but manly and outspoken in his sentiments, which, unhappily, are not politically in full accord with those of General Lee's staff surgeons, one of whom, we are told, is a prominent member of that association.

This may account in a measure for the virus of some of

the accounts sent out adverse to the new cancer cure, which Dr. Bliss has been trying with what he claims to be excellent results. We have already given the claims on both sides, respecting the cundurango, and need not repeat them. As to the expulsion, it is really an honor for which the Doctor is to be congratulated.

There is no record of Bliss ever championing physicians of color or of ever being discriminated against because he came from a Northern state. Once again, poor journalism was supporting Bliss's con. He then took his case to the *Washington Chronicle*.

D. W. Bliss . . . denounces as false and slanderous the statement that he "has diligently published for selfish ends, extravagant accounts of the marvelous efficiency of this South American product, knowing it at the same time to be utterly worthless." He also denies that he refused to cooperate with the medical society in testing its virtues.

The DC Medical Association had wanted statistical evidence of the cundurango cure's success rate, which could only be done by administering it to patients and comparing their outcomes with that of a control group of patients that did not get the cure. Bliss turned down this opportunity to prove scientifically that he was right.

Throughout the fall of 1871, the controversial cundurango cure held the attention of many in Bliss's Grand Rapids community and around the country as well. On October 6, the *Grand Rapids Eagle* reprinted a story originally carried in the *Chicago Tribune*:

A citizen of high standing took his wife, who had been long afflicted with cancer, to Washington, to be treated by Dr. Bliss. Her case was a very serious one, indicating a speedy termination in one way or the other. She tried the cundurango remedy, and patiently waited the result. In less than two weeks, the cancer exhibited alarming signs from bleeding. Dr. Bliss could not account for the change, and an immediate operation was resolved upon. The knife soon explained the condition. An immense growth had become entirely separated from flesh, but at the same time, had prevented the latter from healing, and the flow of blood was from unhealed flesh. As soon as the cancer was removed, the flesh beneath was found apparently free from disease. Comparatively little pain resulted from the operation. The lady rapidly recovered her strength and is now at her home in [Chicago], not only free from every sign or symptom of cancer, but enjoying a degree of health to which she has been a stranger for years.

The theory is that cundurango had the effect to uproot and throw-off the cancerous growth, which had attained large proportions.

A more likely theory is that the cancer Bliss discovered was benign.

Although now a professional pariah, Bliss felt strongly enough about cundurango and continued to defend its merits. Whether he really believed cundurango worked or it was a con, Bliss would not be proven wrong. His professional reputation was at stake.

While in Grand Rapids in early October visiting his sister, Bliss continued to affirm, with great confidence, his belief that cundurango was "a specific for all scrofulous diseases. He claims that it is simply the best alternative, or blood purifier, yet discovered and upon this he stakes his professional reputation," Bliss told the local paper.[2]

The article went on to explain that Bliss's first knowledge of this miraculous bark came from the Ecuadorian minister at Washington, who at the time was a patient of Dr. Bliss. From him Bliss received a small package of the bark. Once again using his political clout, Bliss took it immediately to the residence of Vice President Colfax, whose mother was then dying of cancer.

"That was the first introduction of the 'Cundurango' as a curative agent in this country," the paper dutifully reported.

At that time Dr. Bliss knew nothing of its medicinal virtues, but advised it to be used on the strength of the information given him by the Ecuador Minister. The case was a desperate one, and he told the Vice President that his mother's life might be saved by the use of the remedy. At least he felt assured it would do no harm—and the result proved that "Cundurango" was a specific for cancer.

Dr. Bliss has now on his books 800 cases of cancer, and 3,000 orders for Cundurango from all parts of the world. He claims the remedy is equally as efficacious for all scrofulous diseases, as for cancer. One of the worst cases of cancer was that of the wife of a prominent Chicago banker. It was a bleeding cancer, and would weigh from 5 to 7 pounds. Eight weeks ago she applied for Cundurango, and on Sunday last, when Chicago was a great and prosperous city, the Doctor attended this lady to church, and she stated to him that her health was better than it had been for years.[3]

According to the *Grand Rapids Eagle*, there were still other miraculous cures for which Bliss was responsible.

The wife of a prominent physician of Buffalo, who was dying of cancer, wrote privately and secretly to New York for a small quantity of Cundurango. She commenced taking it without the knowledge of her husband, and in the course of a few weeks commenced growing better. We saw a letter from this lady's husband, addressed to Dr. Bliss, acknowledging the facts, and ordering more of the Cundurango, and confessing that its merits were marked and its curative powers surprising. As we have said, the Doctor only claims that this remedy is simply a blood purifier, and the best yet discovered, and he predicts that in a few years it will be in universal use by the medical profession.

None of the reporters who covered cundurango asked Bliss why his patient, the Minister of Ecuador, would entrust him with valuable financial information regarding how much cundurango was growing on his land. Did Bliss have a financial stake? Was he a partner with the Ecuadorian minister in selling the product in the United States?

"As to the report set afloat by the correspondent of the *Cincinnati Gazette* to the effect that the Minister of Ecuador owned the only accessible lands where the Cundurango could be procured, and that he, with other interested parties was striving to introduce it for speculative purposes, the Dr. declares that the Minister does not own an acre of land there, if anywhere."[4]

Making money was clearly one of Bliss's goals with his quackery. He advertised in major magazines like *Vanity Fair*: "Cundurango! The wonderful remedy for Cancer, Syphilis, Scrofula, Ulcers, Salt Rebum, and All Other Chronic Blood Diseases." The reader was advised to write for the product, care of "Bliss, Keene & Co., Grand Rapids, Michigan."[5]

• • •

Following his expulsion from the Washington medical society, Bliss returned to Grand Rapids and resumed his practice in the city. Completely repudiated by the medical community, the "cundurango cure" eventually disappeared. The negative publicity had been too much, that and the absence of any validated cures.

But with its disappearance, so went the controversy attached to Bliss's involvement with the product. Once again, he avoided ruin. Now he just needed something to get his reputation back. And, once again, history was going to oblige.

14

"Be Always Sure You Are Right, Then Go Ahead"

1872

James Garfield had in front of him as difficult a task as any he had ever been handed as a soldier.

During the war, he had put his life on the line to free enslaved black men and women. Now, in peacetime, he was a member of Congress, tasked with trying to stop the federal government from committing the mass murder of Indians. Garfield's task had been made even more difficult by President Andrew Jackson, who had blazed the Trail of Tears with their bodies.

In 1829 gold had been discovered on Cherokee land in the western Georgia mountains. Though they had no legal right to be there, miners and settlers came from all over to exploit what was not theirs. By the next year, tensions were about to boil over into a full-fledged Indian war. The commercial interests were fortunate enough to have an old Indian fighter in the White House.

As a militia general in 1813, Andrew Jackson had fought the Creeks in Alabama. By his side was a charismatic frontiersman from Tennessee, who named his rifle "Old Betsy."[1] Seventeen years later when Jackson was president, he decided he could really do something about the people he considered savages and help white commercial interests in the process.

Jackson decided to start by banishing Georgia's Cherokee, and then other tribes, from their lands, so that whites could take the gold and everything else on and in it. Jackson therefore championed the Indian Removal Act of 1830. If Congress passed it, which was likely, the president would be allowed to forcibly remove the Indians in the South and relocate them, at the end of bayonets, to unsettled land west of the Mississippi River.

Standing in Jackson's way was that charismatic frontiersman from the Creek War.

Representative David "Davy" Crockett of Tennessee was virulently against the Indian Removal Act. As a frontiersman, Davy believed all his life that justice was due every Indian tribe. So Davy Crockett went to Congress.

Crockett spoke to his colleagues on the floor of the House: "I have always viewed the native Indian tribes of this country as a sovereign people. I believe they had been recognised [sic] as such from the very foundation of this government, and the United States were bound by treaty to protect them; it was their duty to do so. These poor remnants of a once powerful people, their only chance of aid was at the hands of Congress. Should its members turn a deaf ear to their cries, misery must be their fate."[2]

Davy Crockett was the only member of the Tennessee delegation to vote against the Indian Removal Act. It passed Congress by a wide margin. Davy's response to losing?

"You may all go to hell and I will go to Texas."

In ensuing years, not only the Cherokee but the Choctaw, Muscogee, Seminole, and Chickasaw nations were forcibly removed from Georgia and relocated west of the Mississippi River. Because of these brutal forced marches west, it became known as the Trail of Tears.

As time went on, Davy Crockett's prophecy became true—misery and death was the fate of America's indigenous people. Forty-two years later, James Garfield was called on to take up their losing cause.

• • •

The Salish (Flathead) Indians had lived in Montana's Bitterroot Valley for as long as they could remember. Under a previous treaty, the government had given them that land. They had to give permission to any whites who entered. The valley was big, and Chief Victor had 550 in his tribe.

At first, Victor welcomed some settlers. But that led to more settlers, who realized the valley's commercial possibilities in land and agriculture. Then gold was discovered and gold camps sprang up in the valley. Victor's friendliness had backfired on him. W. J. McCormick, special Indian agent for the Salish people, wrote in a report of 1868: "The whites were permitted [by the Federal government] to occupy the most eligible portion of the valley for agricultural purposes. Fields were enclosed, houses and barns were built, until now almost the entire valley presents a spectacle of thrift and agricultural prosperity rarely equaled or met with in any of the new states or territories."[3]

Three years later, the whites were so firmly established that there was no way they would give up the valley. President Ulysses S. Grant decided that the only solution was to do what President Andrew Jackson had done: the government would take the lands by force and kick the Native peoples out to another reservation of the government's choosing.

The man chosen to do the president's bidding was James Garfield. Eight years in office, he had risen to be head of their party. Garfield knew to choose his political battles wisely. If he turned Grant down, someone else would take the job, someone who was not as determined as he was to save the Salish from extinction and get them a good deal.

Garfield knew what the former commanding general of the Union army was capable of militarily. If the Salish people did not move to a new Flathead reservation voluntarily, Grant would send in Lt. Col. George Armstrong Custer to wipe them out. Custer had wiped out the Cheyenne village of Chief Black Kettle in 1868. Of 103 killed, "92 [were] squaws, children and old men."[4]

Since the war, Custer had graduated from killing Confederate soldiers to slaughtering innocents. Garfield was determined not to give Custer the opportunity for another one of his now legendary charges. Negotiation was better than war. Custer didn't care whether he lost any of his men as long as he killed the enemy. That's the way he had been taught at West Point.

But General James Garfield had been taught in battle. And he was a preacher. Each person's life was sacred.

From the communiqués coming back to Washington from the Bitterroot Valley, it was clear that the Flathead were angry; the chiefs did not want their people to move. If Garfield was not successful in negotiating a peaceful end to the conflict, the only resource for Grant was war. That meant the tribe would become extinct.

Grant had put Garfield in the most difficult situation of his life. The Salish people owned the Bitterroot Valley. And they didn't want to move to a reservation. But if they didn't, Grant would annihilate them. Despite the odds, Garfield was determined to save them. Appointed as Special Commissioner for the Removal of the Flathead from the Bitter Root Valley, he saddled up.

To get to Montana, Garfield headed west out of Washington on a train. On August 9, he wrote this eloquent entry in his diary: "9. FRIDAY. Past the cultivated portions of Kansas and the evening reached the desolate plains of Kansas. Buffalo skeletons are seen here and there along the road and the short buffalo grass."[5]

The previous winter, a group of buffalo hunters had hunted the animals for their hides in that area. Getting the animals in their sights, the hunters—including eighteen-year-old William Barclay "Bat" Masterson and his lifelong friend, twenty-three-year-old Wyatt Berry Stapp Earp—raised their .52-caliber Sharps buffalo rifles and fired.[6]

After the animals went down with a huge thud, the hunters gutted them and took their prized skin. The skeletons were left to the buzzards. Garfield was looking at them now. As he traveled west, he also saw what an unforgiving country this could be, in a pure, beautiful, untouched wilderness. On August 22, Garfield reached Montana's Bitterroot Valley and met with the Flathead. "Held a counsel of six hours duration with the chiefs.

Found them greatly opposed to leaving the Bitterroot Valley," he wrote in his diary.

But in his official report for the Department of the Interior, Garfield got more specific. "They insisted that [by the previous treaty] the President was required to have the Bitter Root Valley carefully surveyed and examined."

It hadn't been done.

> They insisted that such a survey and examination should have been made immediately after the ratification of the treaty . . . that for seventeen years no steps had been taken in regard to it, and they considered the silence of the Government on this subject an admission that the valley was to be their permanent home.
>
> They further called attention to the fact that they had learned something of civilization, and done a good deal in the way of cultivating the land and making the valley a more desirable place. All the speakers concluded by claiming the Bitter Root Valley as their home [and] were wholly unwilling to leave it. They however affirmed their steady friendship for the whites and disclaimed any hostile intentions; declaring themselves willing to suffer, peaceably, whatever the Government should put upon them, they would not go to the reservation.[7]

It was a key moment. Garfield knew what Grant would do if the Flathead didn't move. Custer and the Seventh Cavalry would get another opportunity to charge into an Indian village, guns blazing. How many hundreds of women and children would be massacred? Garfield's report continued:

> I did not feel authorized to intimate to them that the Government would force them away, though I was careful not to say it would not. I closed the interview by requesting a direct answer to the question, whether they had decided to disobey the order of the President and the act of Congress, and requested them to take time for consultation and give

me their answer the next morning. I also requested the chiefs to accompany me to the Jocko reservation, that we might together discuss its fitness as their place of settlement.

To refuse meant death. To negotiate meant life. Garfield was trying to make the Flathead an offer they could not refuse. And he was going to make sure they got a good deal. The next morning, the chiefs asked Garfield to assure the president of their good will. They would accompany him to the reservation to which the government wanted to remove them, but that didn't mean they had agreed to leave, at least not yet.

The August 24 entry in Garfield's diary vividly tells what happened next: "SATURDAY. Our party reached the Jocko Reservation 30 miles distant about 2 o'clock P.M. It is a country of wonderful beauty. All the varieties of mountain, valley, prairies and woodland combined. In the afternoon went hunting and fishing. A few grouse, a broken wagon and a five pound trout lost off my hook were the principal events of the afternoon," he wrote with self-deprecating humor.

And then he got down to business: "The chiefs arrived after sunset, and entertained us with a war dance accompanied by heroic recitals of the achievements of the Flat Heads against their enemies the Crows, Sioux and Snakes. These customs are very effective in keeping up the pride and warlike spirit of the tribe."

Garfield's diary entries of August continue:

25. SUNDAY. Had a long conference with the Flat Head and after almost failing, succeeded.

26. MONDAY. Two of the chiefs, second and third, signed the contract, by which they agreed to remove their tribe to the Reservation, when suitable buildings have been erected to receive them, they have selected sites for their dwellings and the grounds for their farms. All the money appropriated for their removal is to be paid for them to fitting up their dwellings.

Yes, the Flathead would have to relocate, but it would be to fertile land, on which the government would build them houses and help them stake out farms. Further, instead of money being used to remove them, that is, to fit out an expedition to relocate them by force, those monies would be given to the Flathead (see the appendix for details of this treaty).

By skillfully using the power of the government without *threatening* to use it, James Garfield saved the tribe from extinction while allowing them their dignity. Now that he had concluded the treaty successfully, Garfield started for home. He was in the wilderness and once again, it would take weeks and all kinds of conveyance to get back home.

> 27. TUESDAY. Took the stage a little after two in the morning for Deer Lodge. [This] beautiful river has been permanently ruined by the miners; and has been for three years as muddy as the Missouri. Before the discovery of gold, it was clear and pure as any mountain stream could well be.

Garfield had just seen with his own eyes the greed of the white man, what it could do to a mountain stream as well as a Native tribe. What he wanted most of all was to get home. Two weeks later, he finally did.

> [September] 11. WEDNESDAY. At 7:00 o'clock this morning, the odor of petroleum filled the cars and informed us we were reaching the suburbs of Cleveland. In five minutes after our train stopped at the Great Atlantic and Western Depot, we were on the train toward home. At [town of] Solon, I was joined by Mother and Harry and Jimmie. At ten past ten were home in Hiram.[8]

Garfield was safe in the bosom of his family. He had done his job and, at least for a while, had saved the lives of the Flathead people through smart, careful negotiation tinged with humanity. He had followed Davy Crockett's motto—"Be always sure you are right, then go ahead."

15

"We Should Not Speak of Love"

While James Garfield was relaxing at home with his family in Hiram, Ohio, after his Montana excursion, thousands of miles east, in Boston, Massachusetts, Alexander Graham Bell had his hands full, doing the same thing that had cost Abram Garfield his life.

"The fire began at 83–85 Summer Street, in the basement of a commercial warehouse at the corner of Kingston Street, downtown," Bell later wrote his mother, Eliza, in Brantford, Ontario. By the time Engine Company 7 arrived, the building was completely ablaze. Attempts to throw water on it failed as the fire continued to spread.[1]

In writing to his father, Melville, Bell reported:

I was in common with half the male population of Boston, out all night on Saturday [fighting the fire]. Fire broke out again today and is now raging. More [buildings] destroyed than in Chicago. I am dead tired so will turn in. I shall write you with full details in the [Boston] Globe newspaper. Look out for the account of an eyewitness account signed A.G.B. And buy some copies.

Your affectionate, Alec[2]

Bell did write an eyewitness account of the fire. He sent it in to the *Boston Globe*. Either the paper didn't like it or it was lost. It never ran. But Bell's letter to his mother makes it clear that when confronted with danger to his own self, he instead served others. He felt a responsibility to the people and the city that he had made his home.

When the chips were down, Bell had proven himself a man of action.

Once the fire was quelled and the city began its recovery, Bell went back to his new life in the United States. He thirsted for a wife. He felt his life would be complete with one. At the same time, he had all these ideas. All of this was on his mind when Gardiner Hubbard, the wealthy businessman his father had met when he was in Boston, engaged him.

Hubbard had a sixteen-year-old daughter, Mabel. She had been deaf since she was five, when rheumatic fever had stolen her hearing. Mabel could not hear her own voice. She needed help communicating. Bell agreed to meet her. When he came to their home, Bell figured his "wife" problem was solved. It was love at first sight of his new pupil. Mabel was more realistic: "He was tall and dark, with jet-black hair and eyes, but dressed badly and carelessly," she later said. "I could never marry such a man!"

Bell figured that if he had money, it would make him a more marriageable prospect. It had worked for other men, why not for him? With an immigrant's perspective, Bell noticed that here in America, he could make big money with an invention. And he had an idea for one. He began to experiment with multiple telegraphy.

At the moment, Samuel Morse's telegraph only allowed one-way communication. The idea was to invent a means of sending multiple signals on the same wire, simultaneously. Until he could create an invention that was patented and made money, Bell needed a way to finance his experiments. He had to pay for room and board, not to mention tobacco for his pipe.

Which is what led him to Salem, Massachusetts. By the time he got there, the witches had already left. What he did encounter was a second private pupil, George Sanders. George's father was a rich leather merchant, who could afford to hire Bell to teach his son Visible Speech. Bell commuted between Boston, where he kept up his work and relationship with Mabel, and Salem.

"He [George] was born totally deaf, and has never spoken a

word in his life. He has never been to school," Bell wrote about his new five-year-old pupil.

Bell moved into a room in George Sanders's grandmother's house in Salem. He proceeded to use Visible Speech to help George communicate. He labeled every object in George's room. Then he put a card file in a corner of the room, bearing the same words.

"George would make his appearance in the morning anxious for play, making vigorous signs for some of his most valued toys. For instance, he would fold his arms and beat his shoulders rapidly with his hands. This was his sign for 'doll.' The doll was accordingly produced, and his attention was directed to the word 'doll' upon it."[3]

Bell taught young George the alphabet, with a glove, on which was written every letter of the alphabet. By touching letters and relating them to his signage, George learned to spell and further communicate.

"The use of the glove alphabet was so little noticeable that I could talk to him very freely without attracting the attention of others. I took him to [P. T.] Barnum's museum and talked to him all the time the lions were being fed."[4]

Barnum, who had vehemently opposed slavery, had a museum in New York City that included lions, bears, and tigers, along with his legendary exhibitions of human oddities, sometimes known as "freaks." Bell and young George looked on with wide eyes at Chang and Eng, the Siamese twins; Anna Swann, the giantess; and General Tom Thumb, a midget.

Bell and his pupil communicated with the magic glove the entire time. Soon, George's learning rate and new-found eloquence stunned his parents. Under Bell's tutelage, the boy could now write letters: "I have a new doll. The dolls are sitting in Mary's chair here. . . . I must not go near the horse because the horse is large and I may go near the cow. I slept in the train from Canada, but now I am in Salem," eight-year-old George wrote his parents in 1874.

Bell, meanwhile, was working on his multiple telegraphy

idea. He tried to get patent protection for it, but failed because he had yet to finish constructing it. He then tried patenting his invention in Britain. Bell's native country turned him down too, this time because he was an absentee citizen. So he used these failures as a learning experience.

He decided to stop work on the telegraph and instead turn to inventions that would aid his teaching, which specifically dealt with human speech. Bell returned briefly to his parents' home in Brantford, Ontario. There, during the summer of 1874, he did a lot of thinking. Combining his knowledge of sending multiple tones over the wires, along with that of teaching the deaf, he came up with the idea for the telephone.

Bell needed a financial backer, someone not only to finance his experiments until he was successful but help him with the business end of things too. He found both right under his nose—Mabel's father, the wealthy Gardiner Greene Hubbard. While continuing to give Mabel speech lessons—as he further tried to ingratiate himself into her heart—Mabel's father financed Bell's work.[5]

The young Scot was putting together a team to help him succeed. And he needed one more member. Bell found the man he needed—Thomas A. Watson. In 1875, the young machinist became Bell's assistant. The two men really hit it off. Watson's father was a livery stable operator in Salem. So the two men were up many a night with their experiments.[6]

Despite Bell's inspired idea for the telephone, Hubbard figured they could make quicker cash if they beat out competing inventor Elisha Gray on the patent for multiple telegraphy. Bell finished his multiple telegraph and thought he was going to be successful when he and Hubbard were invited to the Western Union office, downtown on Broadway in Manhattan.

Bell demonstrated his invention for the company's president, William Orton. When he had successfully transmitted two signals over the same wire simultaneously, Orton asked Bell into his office, alone. There, he threatened to ruin him.

Elisha Gray's invention was similar to Bell's. Unless Bell caved to the financial demands of Orton and his company, Western Union would instead do business with Gray. Because of Western Union's monopoly on telegraphy, Bell's device, though superior to Gray's, would be doomed to history's scrap heap.

Alexander Graham Bell didn't like somebody threatening him, He didn't care who it was. As he met up with Hubbard and they headed out onto Broadway, he told Hubbard of Orton's threats. The March wind stung just a little bit more. The two men realized they had been the victims of industrial espionage. What William Orton had not counted on was that Bell didn't take crap from anybody.

The next day, Bell went back down Broadway and found the Western Union president in his office. He accused Orton of spying on his invention. The idea of the previous day's charade had evidently been for him to show Orton what he had invented so that Western Union could steal it and give it to Gray, who Orton had in his pocket.

As for Orton's disdain of Hubbard, before they even met, he had known damn well that Bell was partners with Hubbard; that was no surprise. Orton never meant to purchase Bell's invention. He just wanted to see what he—and Gray—could steal.

When he left New York City that day, Bell realized that he was through with multiple telegraphy. He began to think more and more about the telephone. It was time to put his ideas into practice and to make certain that this time, nobody could steal his idea. But as he and Watson got down to business, Bell found his attention distracted elsewhere.[7]

Bell was giving Mabel a Visible Speech lesson when he told her how sweet her voice sounded. She could not hear it. But his comments touched her heart.

"Mr. Bell said today my voice is naturally sweet," she wrote her mother after that lesson.[8]

Bell told his family, and everyone else who would listen, that he loved Mabel Hubbard.

"She is beautiful, accomplished, belongs to one of the best families in the states and has the most affectionate disposition that it has been my lot to come across. Her deafness I felt to be a great bar. Her youth too (she is only 17) rendered it unlikely that she would reciprocate my feelings. One difficulty . . . was the fact of my looking so much older than I am. Not one of the family thought me less than 36 until I informed them I was 28," Bell wrote his mother, Eliza.

Bell had spoken to Mrs. Gertrude Hubbard and told her of his love for her daughter. Mrs. Hubbard thought that considering her daughter's tender age, Bell should consider waiting a year before confessing his true feelings. That would give Mabel time to mature into a woman of her own mind. He agreed, finding it terribly difficult and distracting to continue teaching his pupil with his unrequited secret love held in his breast.[9]

That spring, Dom Pedro II, the emperor of Brazil, visited the Boston School for the Deaf, where Bell also taught occasionally. Sporting a long, carefully trimmed white beard, Dom Pedro was an emperor in name only. It just happened that by an accident of birth, he had inherited the throne. A great admirer of Abraham Lincoln's, he was the standard bearer in his own country for freedom of speech and other civil rights.

Dom Pedro was an intelligent man, always interested in new ideas and technologies. He and Bell discussed Visible Speech. He was fascinated by it. The emperor asked Bell to send him Melville's books, so he could read up on it. Bell of course complied readily.

That summer, Bell wrote Mabel of his feelings for her. His heart had made his head realize that he could not go for a whole year without contacting her.[10] She was vacationing on Nantucket Island, a favorite summer place for wealthy New Englanders. Instead of writing back to him, Mabel sent a letter to her mother, which Gertrude Hubbard shared with Bell. Mabel said she wasn't interested. Gertrude, however, was smarter than her underage daughter.

Gertrude decided to lobby for the man she thought would make her daughter a great husband and herself a great son-in-law. Family was important to Gertrude. Mabel finally broke down and wrote to Bell directly on August 30, 1875: "Perhaps it is best we should not meet awhile now, and that when we do meet we should not speak of love. It is too sacred and delicate a subject to be talked about much and till I know what that means myself, I cannot understand or fully sympathise with the feeling. Only if you ever again need my friendly help and sympathy it is yours."[11]

Bell took away the positive from the letter. Mabel wasn't cutting him off. Maybe if he was successful at inventing the telephone and made some money doing it, he'd have what he needed to get married. Bell was staking his happiness on creating an invention that he hadn't even begun to construct yet.

16

"Aye, There's the Rub"

Despite James Garfield's attempt to stave off the slaughter of the Plains tribes, his old commander was determined to do the direct opposite.

The Senate had held hearings regarding corruption in the Bureau of Indian Affairs. The bureau was run by Orville Grant, the president's brother. Garfield watched the hearings from the House chamber next door. There were charges that Indian agents were stealing provisions meant for the tribes, selling the stuff on the side to make money, while the tribes starved. The star witness was Lt. Col. George Armstrong Custer. Custer implicated Orville Grant in schemes to defraud the government, which cheated the Indians. The president did not take the matter of attacking his brother lightly. In retaliation, he removed Custer for a full year from command of the Seventh Calvary, reinstating him in the spring of 1876.

That winter, a renegade band of Sioux, led by Sitting Bull, had left their reservation. Starvation is not entirely conducive to peace. The Sioux were going off reservation to hunt for survival. The government's response was to designate them as federal fugitives. The Sioux would now be hunted as criminals.

Custer was part of a three-pronged attack to bring them to ground. It was supposed to be a coordinated battle. Custer, of course, was not into coordination. What the Boy General really wanted to do, though, was attend the Philadelphia Centennial Exposition, which had recently opened. He hoped that the Seventh Cavalry would take care of the Sioux post haste, so he could get on the first train headed back east and get to Philadelphia. Who knew what marvels he might see at the exposition?

While Custer was making plans for his excursions against the Sioux at Fort Lincoln, North Dakota, where the Seventh Cavalry was stationed, Philadelphia's Centennial Exposition opened on May 10 without him. The previous year, Garfield had been hesitant to vote to fund it, as it was an *international* world fair. As chair of the House Appropriations Committee, Garfield wondered why the United States should pay for something that did not uniquely celebrate the greatness of America. Why should Americans pay money to celebrate other cultures and countries? Eventually, Congress voted to give the exposition planners three hundred thousand dollars of federal funds, not the three million they had asked for.

James and Crete Garfield were there on opening day.

> Crete and I ... sat on the stand in front of the Art Hall and witnessed the imposing ceremonies of the opening of the Exposition. . . . Nearly one hundred thousand people witnessed the ceremonies. But more than the sight of crowds and of titled officials, I was impressed by the grandeur of the human voice when the thousand trained singers rendered in solemn and beautiful music Whittier's [Centennial] hymn.
>
> Crete and I went to the Art Gallery ... [then] through the crowd to Machinery Hall ... Just at the door we met the President with [the] Empress of Brazil on his arm, followed by the Emperor [Don Pedro II] and Mrs. Grant."[1]

June 25, 1876

Custer's scouts had tracked the Sioux to an encampment in Montana's Little Bighorn Valley. After he defeated them, it would only take a scout two days ride from there to the Bozeman, Montana, Territory telegraph office. A telegram would only take two days to reach St. Louis, where the Democrats were having their presidential nominating convention.

With his defeat of the Sioux in hand and big headlines coast-to-coast to boot, Custer thought he'd be a viable Democratic presidential candidate. At almost the exact moment that Custer waved his white hat and charged down into the Little Bighorn Valley in Montana, thousands of miles away at the Philadelphia Exposition he had wanted to attend, Alexander Graham Bell walked into the East Gallery.

Where Custer was fearless, Bell was a bundle of jangled nerves.

He was there to demonstrate the telephone. Bell had already patented it, literally hours before Elisha Gray tried to do the same thing. Only Bell actually had an invention that worked in trials, while Gray just had plans for one. This would be the first public demonstration of Bell's invention.

Gray's harmonic and multiple telegraphs were on display at the ornate Western Union exhibit. Just looking at them made Bell feel nervous and anxious. He was having trouble believing in himself: "I am afraid that the effects I can produce will be much feebler than his, as he has every advantage that the Western Union Telegraph Company can give him. My only chance consists in having my apparatus for the transmission of vocal sound a success," he wrote his mother before stepping into the breach.

Bell was a worrier, but this time he had a lot to worry about. His equipment had arrived in Philadelphia with physical damage from the shipping. He had worked against the clock to make the necessary repairs to his telephone apparatus, so he could meet today's presentation deadline.

"If you persevere, success must come," Mabel wrote him reassuringly. "How I miss you. . . . But I am satisfied when I remember where you are. And when you come home, the duty [to create the telephone] will have been done and the opportunity taken hold of."

Bell's absence had made Mabel's heart grow fonder. She had finally realized that she loved Alec. And he knew it from the words in her letter, which just heightened his anxiety about the future in front of him. Yet, she believed in him.

It was hot and humid, the kind of Philadelphia summer day that John Adams kept complaining about in June one hundred years earlier, during the run-up to the July 4, 1776, Declaration of Independence. Adams would still have been complaining if, one hundred years later, he had been one of those inside the exposition's main building. Basically a large well-fitted-out warehouse, the place was stifling.

Elisha Gray was up first.

Before a waiting, hushed audience, Gray demonstrated his inventions. He was able to transmit music over one hundred feet of wire. Everyone heard the song, "Home Sweet Home." Watching and listening, Bell was more impressed than anyone else.

Is this my Waterloo? he wondered.

With such thoughts floating through his mind, Bell was still distracted, when a man sporting a long, carefully trimmed white beard came up to chat with him.

"Thank you for the books you sent me, Mr. Bell," said Emperor Dom Pedro II.

The emperor of Brazil had not only helped to open the exposition with President Grant, he had hung around to see how things went and to take in the attractions. He had spied Bell through the crowd. A proponent of technology, Dom Pedro was very well aware of what Bell was there to do that day. His friend from Boston was up next.

Dom Pedro accompanied Bell up the stairs to the distant East Gallery. The emperor of Brazil had the Scottish immigrant's back. In the East Gallery, Bell's inventions, the multiple telegraph that Western Union tried to steal, and his telephone receivers, had been laid out on a plain, wooden bench. With sweating judges and crowd in attendance, Bell fell back on his teacher's training.

"I then explained the 'Undulatory Theory' and offered to test the transmission of the human voice," he later wrote his parents.

Bell placed one of his two telephone receivers in an adjacent room. The other remained on the workbench. They were connected by electric wire. The head judge, Sir William Thomson, took up his position at the receiver in the East Gallery. Bell went to the receiver in the adjacent room. Back inside the East Galley, people waited.

"Do you understand what I say?"

Listening at his receiver, Sir William couldn't believe his ears. *It was a human voice.*

"Do you understand what *I* say?" he responded with incredulity. "Where is Mr. Bell? I must see Mr. Bell."

Thomson ran out of the hall, searching for Bell, and found him in the adjacent room.

"Do you understand what I say?" Bell was repeating into the phone, only to look up and see the very man he was talking to beside him.

"I heard the words 'what I say,'" Sir William said breathlessly. "Please sing and recite something."

Sir William ran back to his phone and soon, from out of the invention, he heard Bell's voice over the phone.

"To be or not to be."

Bell had answered the proverbial question. His invention worked. His friend Dom Pedro then took his turn at the receiver. He too listened, as Bell spoke.

"I have heard, I have heard," Dom Pedro exclaimed to the crowd with joy.

Elisha Gray, who had conspired with Western Union to use Bell's ideas for Gray's multiple telegraph, had been watching. When Dom Pedro relinquished it, Gray took up position at the phone.

"Aye, there's the rub," he heard Bell say from the next room.

For Gray, it was just that. Forced to admit in public that Bell had bested him, he turned to the crowd and repeated the words he had just heard. The crowd cheered. Bell had successfully transmitted human speech through an electric wire! That still did not stop Gray from trying to destroy Bell's invention.

The next day, Gray told the judges that Bell's telephone was acoustic, the equivalent of two tin cans tied together by string. It wasn't possible that his voice had been carried by an electric current. It didn't work. But it was Gray's perfidy that did not work; not this time. Bell had proven it scientifically: for the first time in history, the human voice had been transmitted over an electric wire.[2]

As he left the exposition that afternoon, Bell's thoughts turned to the challenge of marketing his invention, making money from it, and hopefully marrying Mabel Hubbard. While Bell pondered what was now beginning to look like a bright future, in Montana, George Armstrong Custer came to the end of his.

Custer's body and those of the 272 men serving with him were lying dead and mutilated, strewn along the banks of the Little Bighorn River, up a hill to a rise where he and a few of his men had made a last stand against the combined force of Sioux and Cheyenne warriors, led by the daring Crazy Horse.

Not being a scientist, Custer had been wrong about how long it took a telegraph signal to go from Montana back to civilization in the East. While the bodies were discovered by an army scout on June 28, it was not until July 4 that word of the massacre went out over the Associated Press wires. It reached the exposition in Philadelphia, where Generals Philip Sheridan and William Tecumseh Sherman were in attendance.

Sheridan pooh-poohed that first report as preposterous.

In the spring of 1877, Gertrude and Gardiner Hubbard decided it was time for Mabel and Alec to marry. Bell had been right. The phone had indeed made him a much more marriageable prospect.

"In fact they urge me very strongly to marry at once.... They say that I will never be well and strong until I have someone to look after me," Bell wrote Melville and Eliza.

On July 11, 1877, Alec and Mabel finally married at a small ceremony at the Hubbards' Cambridge, Massachusetts, home. Alec gave his new wife two great gifts: a cross made of pearls and 1,497 shares of Bell Telephone stock. Soon, Mabel got pregnant. Their first daughter, Elsie, was born in 1878. That's when the Bells decided to move to Washington D C.[3]

"I am hardly ever free from colds all winter long in Boston and neither are you," Mabel said to her husband.

Boston was a center of culture and scientific thought. Bell loved the city. But he couldn't deny Mabel, so he rented a house in Washington. At first, he felt out of place, but things changed.

"[Alec] has about stopped rattling at Washington and is beginning to find there are nice and scientific people here," Mabel wrote.[4]

Washington was indeed a beautiful place with many intelligent people, if you eliminate most of the politicians. Bell was also finding himself loving the United States more and more. He decided to apply for United States citizenship when he was eligible.

Bell was living the American dream. He had risen from penniless immigrant to an inventor making money, married and with a child. He was making money. But his greatest invention, one that could immediately save a human life, was in his future. The failed inventor that would wield it, instead of Bell, lived near him.

In 1880 D. W. Bliss moved back to Washington. It had been eight years since his cundurango cure had riled the medical community in the District of Columbia. Many of the people he had riled up were gone and he was allowed to return to the Washington medical community.

Bliss bought a house on F Street Northwest. Besides his wife, Sophia, his son, Ellis, daughters Eleanor and Eugenia Wilburn, Eugenia's husband, George, their son, Paul, and many servants, all occupied the home. Before cundurango had disappeared, Bliss had indeed made a lot of money.

Now all Bliss needed was an historic event to once again assist him in securing his reputation from the scrap heap of history.[5]

17

"Mr. President, Are You Badly Hurt?"

9:30 a.m., Saturday, July 2, 1881

Against the bright blue sky, on that sunny day, it made quite a sight.

Looking up, Robert Lincoln saw a combination of Victorian and Gothic architecture. The place looked like a cross between a church and a government building. Located at the southwest corner of Constitution Avenue and 6th Street Northwest, the Baltimore and Potomac Railroad Station had opened its swinging doors just three years earlier, in 1878.

Running underneath it was Tiber Creek. Because of its location on soft ground, the new station was supported by wooden beams, driven down thirty-five feet. Leading up to the station were newly laid, wide-gauge railroad tracks across the Long Bridge, down Maryland Avenue Southwest, across the National Mall and ending at B Street. A 130-foot train shed spread out across the Mall, leading up to the station and the main lobby.

Robert and other members of the president's cabinet had gotten there earlier than their boss. President Garfield wasn't about to take a holiday without also doing business. He knew the people didn't pay him to vacation. He had to do the president's work. His cabinet was to accompany the president they served on his train travels south, to Long Branch, New Jersey.

Crete Garfield was at their summer place on the Jersey Shore. Her husband was planning to relax there for a little, before heading north to his college reunion at Williams College, in the Berkshire Mountains of Massachusetts. Not a bad place to be in July, the cool north woods, as opposed to hot, sweaty, swampy, smelly District of Columbia.

Since the president wasn't there yet, Robert and his cabinet had gone out to the train platform where they chatted over cigars. Minutes later, outside the depot, James Garfield arrived in a carriage with James G. Blaine.

Blaine, an old congressional friend, served the president as secretary of state. Garfield also had two of his sons with him—fifteen-year-old James Rudolph and eighteen-year-old Harry Augustus. His three other children, fourteen-year-old Mary, eleven-year-old Irvin, and nine-year-old Abram, were with their mother in New Jersey.

Garfield had been elevated to the presidency at the 1880 presidential Republican convention when the party could not agree on a candidate. The voting had been split between rival factions: the Stalwarts and the Half-Breeds. A good many delegates were for Ulysses S. Grant. He had left office shortly after the Philadelphia Exposition closed, only to embark on a continental tour, with a reporter in tow to report his every move.

By the time he returned to America, Grant was more popular than when he had left office, the taint of the Bureau of Indian Affairs scandal no longer on his coattails. Still, he could not muster the delegates he needed to get back to the White House. It was a brokered convention. On the thirty-sixth ballot, Garfield was selected as the compromise candidate with real bona fides.

As always, Garfield had not chosen the office; it had chosen him. He refused to go on the road and campaign for himself, as other presidential candidates did. Instead, Garfield conducted the first "front porch campaign" from his home in Lawnfield, Ohio, where he spoke to voters and reporters.

In the general election, James Garfield's opponent was General Winfield Scott. The general in command when the Union army fell ignominiously at the First Battle of Bull Run, and whom Lincoln had fired, previously ran unsuccessfully for president as the Whig Party nominee in 1852, and lost. Which he was obviously good at doing.

James Garfield was elected twentieth president of the United States.

In his inaugural address of March 1881, Garfield spoke of the national significance of full and equal rights for its black citizens: "The elevation of the negro race from slavery to full rights of citizenship is the most important political change we have known since the adoption of the Constitution of 1776. No thoughtful man [or woman] can fail to appreciate its beneficent effect upon our people. It has freed us from the perpetual danger of war and dissolution; it has added immensely to the moral and instructional force of our people; it has liberated the master as well as the slave from a relationship which wronged and enfeebled both."[1]

Only three months later, Garfield was stepping down to the pavement from his carriage in front of the depot. He linked arms with his old friend Blaine and chatted about political things. Then they had to unlink their arms as they went through the swinging doors.

Tracking his quarry was Charles Guiteau. He knew from the newspapers that the president was going to be there, because they published his schedule. Standing in the shadows, just inside the entrance, the little man had an equalizer in his pocket.

Charles Guiteau was hearing voices: "I'll teach you to deny me the office that is rightfully mine! Shoot him!" But it wasn't always that way.

The fourth of six children, Guiteau was born on September 8, 1841. His mother died when he was but five years old. His father, who soon deserted the family, was a dedicated follower of the Oneida Community in New York State in the 1840s. Founded by John Humphrey Noyes, Noyes's doctrine was a self-described "millennial Communism," a strange mixture of biblical prophecy and Karl Marx, with a little free love thrown in.[2]

In 1859 Guiteau's maternal grandfather passed, leaving him a modest inheritance, enough to attend the University of Michigan in Ann Arbor, not far from Grand Rapids, where D. W. Bliss had his practice. Guiteau had hoped to settle into college life. In fact, he was being given the same opportunity, and then some, as the man he would come to hate more than any other. Guiteau did not settle into college life. Growing increasingly melancholy, he turned to Noyes's teachings, as his father had, for solace. He joined the Oneida Community the following year, stayed for five, and still felt unfulfilled. What could he do with his life, he wondered? And why am I always so unhappy? The questions remained unanswered.

Seeking solace, he turned to his brother-in-law, George Scoville, who had married his sister Frances. Guiteau loved her. Frances had raised him after their mother died and their father deserted them. Through the years, she had provided him with both moral and financial support. Scoville invited his brother-in-law to come to work in his Chicago law office. And he would provide room and board.

For once in his life, Guiteau took advantage of an opportunity. He accepted Scoville's kind offer and came to work in Chicago. But once again, Guiteau's melancholy overwhelmed him. He quit his brother-in-law's firm and instead decided to sue the Oneida Community on a trumped-up charge of withholding compensation for the work he claimed to have done for them.

Moving back to New York, he sent a series of blackmailing letters to Noyes, threatening to take physical action, if the money due him was not paid. Guiteau was finally forced to cease and desist when Noyes's lawyers threatened to prosecute him if he continued.

By 1868 he was back in Chicago, where Scoville took him back into his firm, as a law clerk. This time, Guiteau applied himself. He studied for and passed the Illinois bar. Setting up a small private practice, Guiteau, now a full-fledged lawyer, married Annie Bunn, a librarian at a local YMCA. That's when the voices first came. Guiteau obeyed them.

He battered Annie with his fists, then dragged his frightened wife and locked her in the closet of their new Wabash Avenue flat. Guiteau did this for seven days in a row. But Annie had grit. On the eighth day, when he let her out, she waited until he was asleep and then left him forever, soon obtaining a divorce. Guiteau then tried his hand at starting a newspaper. When that didn't work, he went back to living with his sister Frances and Scoville. One day, Frances went out back, where Guiteau was chopping wood. She passed close to him. That's when he suddenly raised the ax overhead, with the full intent of bringing it down upon her head.

Years later, Frances would remember gazing up at her brother's face, angry and red. She could see the ax blade poised in the air, ready to strike her down. Frances made a break for it, just as the ax came down toward her head and into the space she had recently occupied. She kept running. So did Guiteau. He dropped the ax and ran.

He kept running for the next two years, when he reappeared in his new guise as an itinerant preacher. When that too didn't work, he decided to get into politics. Guiteau had always been interested in politics.

In 1880 he became involved in the Republicans intraparty conflict between the Stalwart faction, led by Roscoe Conkling, and the Half-Breeds, led by James G. Blaine. At first Guiteau had sided with the Stalwarts. But then, James Garfield (who voted with the so-called Half-Breed faction) became the brokered candidate on the thirty-sixth ballot at the 1880 Republican convention.

Guiteau changed sides and moved to Washington DC, to help get Garfield elected. Working hard, passing out pamphlets door-to-door, Guiteau figured he was owed something when James Garfield was elected president. Like so many others, he felt he was owed a political sinecure for helping elect the president—for passing out pamphlets door-to-door.

Guiteau got an appointment and went to the White House to meet with the president and press his case. Pretty much anyone could do that in those days. Meeting with those who wanted patronage was part of the chief executive's job. It was a system Garfield had presently to deal with but was determined to reform.

Waiting outside the president's office, Guiteau was finally summoned inside, where he found James Garfield behind the same desk that had once belonged to Lincoln (although Garfield had taken down Jackson's portrait and replaced it with the rail-splitter's). There was also a telephone on the desk, the first president to have one in the White House. Since his younger days, Garfield's hairline had receded and he had put on a little weight around the middle. But his beard was dark and he was still in great physical shape.

What Guiteau wanted was the Gray Ghost's job, or one like it.

After the War Between the States, John Singleton Mosby, the famous Confederate guerrilla fighter, known by the sobriquet the Gray Ghost, became a passionate supporter of the Union and campaign manager for his old adversary, Ulysses S. Grant. When elected to the presidency, Grant made Mosby counsel to Hong Kong.

In reviewing his predecessors previous appointments, Garfield let John Singleton Mosby keep his job.[3] Guiteau, though, did not have the Gray Ghost's Republican bona fides. Nor did he present a picture of confidence. Whatever was said between them, when the interview was over, Guiteau felt that his chances of getting an appointment were over too. Garfield was giving him the brush-off.

Which was why Guiteau went to the train station when he heard the president was leaving Washington. He wanted revenge. When he saw Garfield entering with Blaine, the little man raced from the shadows. Guiteau pulled from the waistband of his trousers, kept up by a loose pair of galluses, a Belgian-made, .44-caliber Bulldog pistol that he'd recently bought for ten dollars.

Guiteau pulled back the hammer on the short-barreled revolver, then pulled the trigger. The pistol report echoed off the lobby's walls as a loud "bang." Without time to complete a thought, Garfield turned, suddenly feeling a sting in his shoulder, where the bullet had just grazed him.

Surprised by the Bulldog's heavy recoil, Guiteau had been

knocked off balance, which accounted for that first bullet going awry. The Bulldog was inaccurate at ranges beyond sixty feet, as it only had a front sight. Determined not to fail, Guiteau moved forward to get into the pistol's twenty-foot firing range.

Garfield turned.

"My God, what is this?" Garfield shouted, not recognizing the little man with the baleful stare, who had sought a counselor position from him days before at the White House.

Eying the revolver leveled point blank at him, Garfield turned to flee. Guiteau fired a second time. The bullet smashed into Garfield's back. Dr. Robert Reyburn, a professor of anatomy and surgery at Howard University, was nearby. As the president fell, Guiteau dropped the gun and ran for the exit. He was stopped by a police officer before he left. Giving up without a struggle, he was arrested and taken to the station house.

Hurrying over, Reyburn knelt down on the sawdust-covered floor of the station, the blood congealing under Garfield and milling with the sawdust, turning it from yellow to red. Garfield knew exactly what was happening. He was completely conscious.

"Mr. President, are you badly hurt?" Reyburn asked.

"I am afraid I am," said Garfield calmly.[4]

18

"It Was a Time of Intense Excitement and Painful Suspense"

Despite what had happened to him in Jersey City, Robert Lincoln had no phobias around train platforms. He was still out on the train platform with the others, unaware of the trauma inside the depot, when suddenly, a police officer was running down the platform.

"The president's been shot!" someone shouted.

At that first cry, Robert's spine froze. Recovering quickly, Robert and the cabinet ran after the officer and into the depot. Inside, Robert saw the president "weltering in blood" on the floor of the ladies waiting room in the depot.[1] As soon as he did, his thoughts flew back fifteen years to the Petersen House and his wounded father.

Someone needed to take charge. Robert Lincoln took over. It was just natural. His father was the only president ever shot. That gave him the cachet that he resented, though it would now help others listen to him. He made the decision to remove the president to the White House for further treatment. Garfield's thoughts turned to Crete. He had his private secretary, Colonel Rockwell, send her an immediate telegram.

Mrs. Lucretia B. Garfield

The President wishes me to say to you from him that he has been seriously hurt. How seriously he cannot yet say. He is himself and hopes you will come to him soon. He sends his love to you.

Signed,
Colonel Rockwell[2]

A police ambulance was dispatched to the station. The hooves of the horses pulling the ambulance, containing the president of the United States, set up sparks as they struck the Washington cobblestones in quick succession. The ambulance driver was whipping the horses to get to the White House posthaste. It was followed by throngs of the grieving, wondering if a second president would die at the hands of an assassin's bullet. When they got there, Garfield looked up at the windows of the Executive Mansion. He could see his staff peering out. Smiling, Garfield gave them a crisp military salute.

Robert recalled that Dr. Willard Bliss of Armory Square Hospital had attended his father. He had no knowledge that he and Garfield were old friends, let alone that Bliss had not been allowed by Charles Leale to even touch his father after he was shot. Bliss was summoned to the White House for a third time.

When the ambulance got to the Executive Mansion, Garfield was immediately taken inside and placed on a bed in the residential quarters, about to be made into a hospital sick room. Robert Lincoln telegraphed for a special train to pick up Crete Garfield in New Jersey and convey her down to Washington. As she traveled south to the district, dispatches updating Crete on the president's condition would meet her at every station along the way.

Besides Bliss, Robert then made the decision to call in two more physicians who had treated his father. Sixty-four-year-old Surgeon General Joseph K. Barnes, who had attended Lincoln at Petersen House, was summoned. During the war, Barnes had risen to the rank of brigadier general. He had a quiet, unassuming manner in which he performed his medical duties.

That lack of ego and devotion to his men had gained for Barnes the love and esteem of the soldiers whom he treated.[3] He was such a good surgeon that sixteen years earlier, when it had been time to explore for the bullet in Lincoln's head, he was the one, rather than Bliss, Charles Leale had entrusted with the job. Bliss had never forgotten that.

Dr. Joseph Javier (J.J.) Woodward was next on Robert's list. After serving for a year as a field surgeon with the Second Artillery of the Army of Potomac during the war, Woodward had been promoted in 1862. Sent to Washington, he worked under Barnes in the Surgeon General's office. J.J. had a particular interest in the microscope and photography and later became the father of photomicrography. He had the incredible responsibility of performing the autopsy not only on Lincoln but Booth as well.[4]

But it made no difference who Robert called in and how brilliant they were. As soon as he arrived at the White House, Bliss took charge.[5]

He had learned from Lincoln's assassination. NO ONE was going to shut him out this time. When speaking with Robert, Bliss traded on his "friendship" with the president. Robert agreed to let Bliss call the shots. Bliss would determine the course of the president's treatment, and who was even allowed into the room with the president.

Robert was denied the knowledge that since the day Bliss and Garfield had met on the road to their futures back in Ohio, they had had little or no contact. And he certainly didn't talk about the fact that he never treated Robert's father at Petersen House. Since Robert had been out of President Lincoln's room most of the time, he didn't know any better.

"Mr. President, your old friend from Ohio, Dr. Willard Bliss, has been called in to treat you," Robert told Garfield.

Garfield felt fortunate. Not only was he going to have an "old friend" attending him, Bliss had been one of Lincoln's doctors too. Like Robert Lincoln, Garfield did not know that Bliss had never touched the president. He was, unwittingly, about to entrust his life to the same man who had conned dying people into buying his "cundurango cure," and who had left wounded behind him at Bull Run.

Bliss was one of those doctors who liked to operate. Now that he had finally been given the opportunity to explore for a bullet in the body of the president of the United States, he was going to take it. This time, the OTHERS would watch while HE operated.

In the United States, antiseptic methods for preventing wound infection during patient treatment had not yet been fully accepted. For doctors like Bliss, the dirtier the better. His dirty Nelaton probe snaked its way through Garfield's back, deep enough that it snagged on one of his ribs. After a little jiggling, Bliss got it out. Then he stuck his finger into the wound, pushing further and further.

The blood coated his hands, dripping down his fingers. Bliss formed the opinion that the bullet was close to the president's liver. No matter what, he would not deviate from that conclusion. But while sepsis prevention was not yet an accepted medical practice in the United States, anesthesia administered while operating was.

Yet Bliss used neither ether nor chloroform, commonly used anesthetics, to knock Garfield out. He deliberately kept his "old friend" in intense and unnecessary pain during the entire procedure. At 11:30 a.m., Bliss issued the first official bulletin about how the president was doing. Bliss wasn't about to release any details of the procedure, or anything else for that matter: "The president has returned to his normal condition. Will make another examination soon. His pulse is now 63."

That wasn't true, and Bliss knew it. He was just trying to quiet the press. The country was in an uproar. For the second time in fifteen years, the president of the United States lay wounded from an assassin's bullet. What would happen next? Would this one survive? The last thing Bliss wanted was the truth to get out.

The president's blood pressure was falling; the bullet had yet to be detected. Above all else, Bliss needed to make sure that if the president died, he was not in any way held responsible. An hour later Bliss issued his second bulletin. Bliss's experience manipulating the press now came into play: "The reaction from the shot injury has been very gradual. The patient is suffering some pain, but it is thought best not to disturb him by making an exploration for the ball, until after the consultation at 3 p.m."

Bliss was lying; he had already explored for the bullet when he arrived at the White House. That was a matter of record. He was the one who deliberately put James in pain, by not using an anesthetic. As for consulting with his peers, Bliss wasn't interested in what Reyburn and Barnes had to say. Why were their opinions better than his?

> Executive Mansion, 2:45 p.m.
> No official bulletin has been furnished by Dr. Bliss since 1 o'clock. The condition of the President has been growing unfavorable since that time. Internal hemorrhage is taking place and the gravest fears are felt as to the result.[6]

As the sun was setting over the Potomac River, the next bulletin came out of the White House: "7:35 p.m.—The President this evening is not so comfortable. He does not suffer so much pain in the feet."

Garfield had actually lost feeling in his feet. And his vital signs were not good.

"Pulse, 126; temperature 101.9; respiration 24," the bulletin continued.

With such bad news, Bliss chose now to include Barnes's and Woodward's names on the bulletin with his.[7]

The next day, Crete Garfield arrived via the special train. Immediately brought to her husband's side, Garfield seemed to be rallying. They shared some intimate time together, alone, with Bliss out of the room.

Garfield would bear the pain stoically, no matter how bad. Anything else would detract from the prestige of his considerable office, not to mention diminish confidence in the government. Garfield was also determined to survive. And as word of the attempted assassination spread, it wasn't just the nation watching what happened in Washington. The world was also watching.

Alexander Graham Bell wrote, "It was a time of intense excitement and painful suspense. The prolonged suffering borne so bravely and well by President Garfield must still be fresh in every recollection. The whole world watched by his bedside, and hopes and fears filled every passing hour."[8]

Cables flew into Washington on Independence Day, from all parts of the globe.

Tokyo, July 4, 1881

To Yoshad, Japanese Minister, Washington

The dispatch announcing an attempt upon the life of President Garfield has caused here profound sorrow. In the name of His Majesty, to the Government of the United States, has caused here profound sorrow and you are hereby instructed to convey in the name of his majesty, you the Government of the United States, the deepest sympathy and hope that his recovery will be speedy. Make immediate and full report regarding the sad event.

Wooyeero,
Acting Minister for Foreign Affairs

Bucharest, Catrocinni, July 4, 1881

To President Garfield, Washington:

"I have learned with the greatest indignation and deplore most deeply, the horrible attempt against your precious life and beg you to accept my warmest wishes for your recovery.

[Prince] Charles[9]

Over the next few weeks, the medical bulletins coming out of the White House were filled with the arcane details of the physician's trade—the president's pulse, blood pressure, temperature—anything else Bliss could think to put in to disguise what was really happening: under his care, the president was getting worse.

Unknown to anyone else, except the doctors he kept by the wayside, Bliss kept exploring for the bullet, making the wound bigger and bigger as he did. And always without anesthetic, keeping Garfield in pain. Thomas Francis Pendel, who worked as a guard in the White House, was an eyewitness to what happened next.

19

"Science Should Be Able to Discover Some Less Barbarous Method of Exploration"

White House guard Thomas Pendel recalls in his memoir, *Thirty-Six Years in the White House*, the first few days after Garfield was shot. "The day he was shot and on Sunday he kept talking all the time, but Monday he let up some, and then Tuesday morning [Dr. Bliss] shut down on his talking. Sunday morning, just after the big crowd had cleared away, I was alone with the General and Dr. Bliss. The Doctor sat on one side of the bed and I on the other."

Many people still referred to Garfield as "the General." Garfield took hold of Bliss's hand as a drowning man would of the hand pulling him out of the drink. He turned to Thomas Pendel.

"Do you know where I first saw Bliss?" Garfield asked with a smile.

"No, I don't," Pendel answered.

"When I was a youngster, and started for the college at Hiram, I had just fifteen dollars—a ten-dollar bill in an old leather pocketbook, which was in the breast-pocket of my coat, and the other, five, was in my trousers pocket."

He described how the day was hot, how he took off his coat to cope with the heat, and how he took good care to feel every moment or two for the pocketbook. The hard-earned fifteen bucks was to pay his entrance at the college. His thoughts scattered to the wind, as he got to thinking over what college life would be like, and he forgot all about the pocketbook. And when he finally felt for it again, it was gone.

"I went back mournfully along the road, hunting on both sides for my pocketbook. After awhile I came to a house where a young man was leaning over a gate, and he asked me what I was hunting for. I explained my loss, and described the property, when the young man handed it over."

Garfield was laughing uproariously and concluded his story.

"That young man was Bliss, wasn't it, Doctor?" he said to Bliss.

Bliss laughed.

"He saved me for college," Garfield told Pendel.

"Yes, and maybe if I hadn't found your ten dollars, you wouldn't have been president of the United States," Bliss quickly answered, as if he and Garfield were a vaudeville comedy team.

"If I get well, and make any mistakes in my administration, Bliss, you will have to take the blame," and Garfield laughed again.[1]

Later that year, in a major American magazine, Bliss would deny this conversation took place.

Up in Boston, Alexander Graham Bell was watching the drama unfold from afar. He was vacationing with Mabel at her father's house, where it also gave him an opportunity to discuss business with Gardiner Greene Hubbard. Just five years removed from his greatest achievement, Bell was busy fending off contentious lawsuits from competitors, all claiming they had invented the telephone first. They wanted money, which Bell now had.

The previous year, France had bestowed on him the Volta Prize for inventing the telephone. With the honor came a stipend of fifty thousand francs, about ten thousand American dollars, a veritable fortune. That had financed the Volta Laboratory, which he built in Georgetown, just a few miles from the White House. And that telephone stock he gave Mabel as a wedding present had gone up considerably.

Bell had already used some of his newfound wealth to finance the invention of the photophone, an optical, wireless telephone. He had just conducted successful experiments in magnetic recording, recording sound onto electroplated phonograph records. But all that paled alongside the president's plight.

Bell had come to love America. President Garfield was wounded and perhaps dying. Unless science intervened, he could die. That's when he read about Simon Newcomb. Like Bell, he was an immigrant. He hailed from the same Canadian port at Nova Scotia that Bell had landed in when he first came to the American continent.

In 1871 Newcomb was working as a professor of mathematics at the Washington Naval Observatory, where he became secretary of the American Transit of Venus Commission. The transit of the planet Venus across the Sun was a rare astronomical event that needed to be documented. Part of his job as secretary was to submit a budget for the project to Congress.

Garfield was chair of the powerful House Appropriations Committee at the time, so Newcomb's budget request had come to Garfield's desk. Always interested in science and the progression of human knowledge, Garfield had invited Newcomb over to his Washington residence. They had drinks, dinner, cigars and discussed the universe. Afterward, he steered Newcomb's budget appropriations through his committee.

It turned into an eight-year program that cost the taxpayers $375,000, an inexpensive price for mapping a part of the known universe.[2] Now Newcomb was only too willing to help Garfield when the chips were down.

In the heat and humidity of the July summer, it was particularly oppressive at the White House. Garfield was dehydrating and he could easily die from that. Whether Bliss liked it or not, Colonel Joseph Stanley Brown, the president's personal secretary, had Garfield moved to the cooler North Bedroom. Then Brown sent a note to Simon Newcomb: would he come to the White House and use his expertise to help find a way to cool down the president's body temperature?

Under Bliss's baleful eye, Newcomb and several naval engineers created a device that forced air over ice blocks, effectively lowering the room temperature by twenty degrees Fahrenheit. It was the word's first air conditioner. But he didn't give himself time to pat himself on the back, not when his friend still had that bullet in his back.

Bell had already begun to ponder the problem.

"No one could venture to predict the end, so long as the position of the bullet remained unknown. The bullet might have become safely encysted, but on the other hand, recovery might depend upon its extraction. The search with knife and probe among vital and sensitive tissue would be painful and dangerous. My thought is that that science should be able to discover some less barbarous method of exploration," Bell later wrote.

Bell began to explore the possibility of using electricity and magnetism to get the job done: "The thought occurred that the bullet might produce some sensible effect in modifying the field of induction of a coil, brought near the body of the President, and that the locality of the bullet might thus be determined without danger to the patient and without pain; for it is well known that induction can be powerfully exerted through the human body without producing any sensation whatever."[3]

But his laboratory was back home in Washington; and he was then in Boston.

Needing help with materials and construction, Bell strode over to see Charles Williams Jr., a manufacturer of electrical and telephonic apparatus. Williams generously gave Bell his best assistants to help with his experiments. It didn't help. Where Newcomb had succeeded immediately with his invention, Bell failed in these preliminary experiments to create a machine that could detect a bullet in the human body, or in anything else for that matter.

Nothing was ever easy for Bell. Yet failure seemed to bring out the best in him. He determined not to give up. He would eventually succeed. Now, he knew it! He had invented the phone, hadn't he? A few days later, Bell sat down for breakfast with the morning papers: "I learned from the newspapers that Prof. Simon Newcomb had the idea of using a magnetic needle to indicate by retardation of its rotation the proximity of the bullet in the body of the President. I telegraphed to Prof. Newcomb the offer of my assistance in carrying on experiments, knowing the comparative difficulty he would experience in having apparatus made in Washington."

There was no phone service, yet, between Boston and Washington DC. So over the next few days, Bell was forced to use antiquated technology; they exchanged ideas via telegraph. To Bell's surprise, he found that Newcomb appreciated his ideas: "This appreciation determined me to proceed to my laboratory at Washington, where I was accompanied by Mr. Sumner Tainter," Bell's new assistant.[4]

Newcomb couldn't very well keep Alexander Graham Bell's presence a secret. He was the man who had just invented the telephone, for God's sake; reporters followed his every move. The astronomer had to tell Bliss that he had called in the inventor of the telephone to discuss with him an invention that could painlessly detect the bullet in the president's body, so Bliss could operate without further physical probing.

Bliss could not have been too thrilled.

With the glare of the spotlight on him, Bliss couldn't very well turn down a meeting with the great inventor. Considering his own history as a failed inventor, it must have galled him to have Alexander Graham Bell called in, and not by him. Mabel, too, was also thinking about her husband's visit to the White House.

She had been taught that when you went visiting, you never went empty-handed. Mabel gave Alec a basket of grapes for Crete with the note, "To Mrs. Garfield, a slight token of sympathy from Mr. & Mrs. Alexander Graham Bell." Taking it, and accompanied by Tainter, they got on the train for New York City.

Bell and Tainter got off the train in midtown and then took the elevated railway around the city's western edge. The elevated let them off at a ferry that took them across the Hudson River to Jersey City. They had to do all that because there was no rail tunnel under the Hudson River. You had to go to New Jersey on the mainland to pick up the train south.

As Bell watched the Palisades cliffs during the ferry crossing, his mind wasn't just on the task in front of him, but what lay behind in Boston. Mabel was pregnant with their third child. They needed to hire a nanny, which in their case was very important, since Mabel could not hear. The nanny's job was to act as Mabel's ears.

Getting on the train south in Jersey City, those thoughts fell by the wayside the closer he got to Washington. At the train station, Simon Newcomb met him and Tainter with a carriage. With his dark, flashing eyes and wild white beard that stuck out all over the place, Newcomb looked like a mad scientist. He was anything but.

Simon Newcomb was a genius in his area of expertise, just like Bell was in his. Newcomb, the Canadian immigrant, would eventually be hailed as America's first great astronomer. Pulling through the gate at 1600 Pennsylvania Avenue, their cab stopped in front of the dingy-looking, white building that needed a new coat of paint.

The region south of Constitution Avenue and west of Fifteenth Street was mostly submerged under the Potomac River and the tidal swamps that dotted the shoreline. The Washington Monument, half finished, stood on a peninsula. When it was finished in a few more years, it would rise six hundred feet from its base and commemorate a founding father who had released his slaves when he died.

Looking at the Executive Mansion, Bell saw that its south lawn stretched down to the mosquito-ridden swamps on the river's southern shoreline. Dr. Carlos Finley of Cuba had just brought forth the theory that mosquitoes were carriers of malaria. James Garfield was already infected from his days as a canal boy. But Crete wasn't, until taking up White House residence.[5]

Entering through the Pennsylvania Avenue entrance, Bell's olfactory sense was immediately struck by the sour smell of sewage, wafting through the dank recesses of the building. Raw sewage, including human waste, had been dumped in the river upstream. Drifting downriver, the odoriferous offerings got caught in the swamp reeds.

On a windy, summer's day, you could smell the White House as far south as Fredericksburg.

Bell made sure to give the basket of grapes from Mabel to

Joseph Stanley Brown, the president's private secretary. Then he was taken upstairs. Outside the North Bedroom where the president lay in his sick bed, Bell met with Bliss. He carefully explained the scientific principles of induction balance.[6]

It was a brief conversation. What Bliss took away from it was that the person who wielded the invention was the one who would get the credit for locating the bullet. If it worked. And if it did, Bliss was determined that it would be him. But that also gave him an idea.

After Bell left, Bliss started thinking. If Bell could invent something to try out on the president, why shouldn't he do the same thing? He was an inventor, too, just like Bell. He had created inventions before. The president was having trouble eating. Bliss would invent another way of him taking food, besides through his mouth.

PART THREE

When the legend
becomes fact, print the
legend.

—John Ford's *The Man Who
Shot Liberty Valance*

20

"Papa Has Gone to Make Poor Mr. Garfield Well"

D. W. Bliss wasn't the only one concerned about someone eating food. Mabel Bell was worrying, along with everything else, about what her husband was eating while he conducted his experiments. She had been furiously reading the papers to see what her husband was doing. So she picked up her pen and wrote him a letter.

Saturday, July 16, 1881

My darling Alec:

I cannot begin to tell you how anxiously I watch for news of you and your doings, how you are succeeding. Oh, how I hope you will be able to find the bullet, it would be such a triumph for you. Of course I want it for the President's sake also, but I want you to be the man to do it my own dear boy.

Alec loved Mabel so much. He had been so lucky to find her. And she was such a good writer. Her letter continued.

Your arrival and "Professor" Tainter's was in the papers yesterday, also a full account of what was said to be the instrument you would use. I don't know how correct it was, not very I fancy, for it was given by Professor Newcomb, before your arrival.

She did know about Newcomb's invention to cool the president.

I want to know how you are *personally*, whether you manage to lower the temperature of your laboratory at all. I fancy you are so eager and excited that you don't feel the heat as you otherwise would. Only for my sake, do take care and don't wear yourself all out. I at all events would think the President's life a poor exchange for yours.

Mabel was being realistic. Hardworking men dropped dead all the time of heart attacks. She went on to write how the errands he had given her to do with some local scientists, to get material needed for his invention, had not gone as well as she would have liked.

Cousin Sam has just gone to the mountains. I did feel snubbed yesterday when I apologized for giving him so much trouble about your telegram, and he said he was only too glad to do anything for Mr. Garfield (not your humble servant!).

Mabel could turn a sarcastic phrase when she needed, then shift right back to the personal.

I sent you a nightshirt, shirts, collars, cuffs and handkerchiefs and would have sent more grapes but feared they would be smashed. I will send more on Monday to you care of Brown, White House, so if you leave before they come, you can tell him what they are for.

Ever so much love, Your Mabel.[1]

A letter from Boston to Washington DC could take a few weeks to arrive. Telegrams were faster but of course more expensive. Still, the letter was a better way to express emotion. The next day, while Mabel's letter was in transit, Bell sat down at his desk in the Volta Laboratory to write Mabel a letter, using the nickname he had for her in the salutation.

Sunday, July 17th, 1881.

My dear little May:

How are you getting on? You poor little wifie, I feel so anxious about you. How do you manage about going up and down stairs? Is the doctor still with you? I hope he . . . will remain in the house till I return. And what have you done about nurses? I did not think of Maria as a temporary nurse. I would certainly take her rather than the young girl.

My only objection to Maria was as a permanency on account of her having children of her own to take care of. I think, however, you could not do better than take her, until you get another nurse. Now about self.

He went on to describe his and Tainter's arrival at the White House. Bell had given the grapes to Brown, the president's private secretary. The next day, Brown thanked Mabel and him for the gesture. Then Bell got into specifics about his invention.

We have constructed Balances of different sizes and get better and better results as we reduce the size of the apparatus. We are now constructing coils just the size of the leaden bullet itself and hope for still better effects. Yesterday we were able to locate a bullet held in the clenched hand and last night I located successfully a bullet hidden in a bag filled with cotton-waste. This looks promising. Maximum hearing distance yet obtained— two inches. Nothing further to add, save that I am suffering less from heat than usual.

Kiss for Elsie (x) Kiss for you (X) Kiss for Daisy (x)
Your loving husband, Alec.[2]

July 26, 1881, Late Evening

Nine days later, Bell sat down at his desk in the Volta Laboratory, not many blocks from the White House. He picked up a pen and dipped its metal nub in an ink well. In black ink, he wrote in such strong clear letters that a century later, they were still clearly legible:

ALEXANDER GRAHAM BELL TO MABEL (HUBBARD) BELL
Volta Laboratory, 1221 Conn. Ave.
Washington DC

Tuesday, July 26th, 1881

My Darling:

I owe you a long letter to make up for my epistolary silence. I have telegraphed you every day as a means of easing my conscience but after all, telegrams are not such satisfactory things as letters. They are public, as they have to pass through so many hands en route to their destination.

In the case of my telegrams to you concerning the experiments to locate the bullet in the body of the President, I have no doubt they are all discussed by the employees of the Telegraph company—and thus run a great chance of leaking out into the public Press.

Telegraphers "tipped" news hounds on stories that came over the wires and got paid under the table for that service. It was a secondary consideration that, if William Upton and Western Union ever found out what Bell was up to, they would, again, try to steal his invention, which, again, worked.

Bell's idea had been to take two metal coils and bring them over the suspected site of the bullet. Connected to a bell from his telephone, the ringing of the bell would indicate the metallic bullet had been found. On July 22, Bell used what he termed his "new explorer instrument" to detect an old bullet in the body of an old soldier.

The ringing of the bell was a feeble sound, but it indicated where the bullet was if a surgeon wanted to operate to remove it. In clinical trials on other war veterans who still had lead in their bodies, the explorer, which would also be known as the induction balance, found the lead every time.[3] And with a louder ring.

Bell had created the world's first metal detector, and he intended to use his invention to save the president's life. "I telegraphed you this morning that the Induction Balance would be tried upon the person of the President this evening. . . . And this evening, I sent you a [second] dispatch, not intended for you at all but for the employees of the Telegraph Company to the effect that 'Trial of apparatus on President postponed for a few days,'" Bell continued in his letter to Mabel.

It had been a ruse, a con.

"As a matter of fact, preliminary experiments were made upon the person of the President this evening. I will briefly give you a description of this eventful day."[4]

Bell knew that he was running out of time. He had been periodically informed of the president's deteriorating condition. He had just worked forty-eight hours straight to perfect his invention. He felt tired, ill, dispirited, and headachy and went home to bed thoroughly exhausted on July 25.

Bell didn't get up until eleven o'clock on the morning of July 26. Waiting for him at the breakfast table was a telegram from Mabel.

MABEL (HUBBARD) BELL to ALEXANDER GRAHAM BELL

My dear Alec:

Your two telegrams yesterday were very welcome, though I did want more full accounts of the President, as they were all the news we could get since morning and we were very anxious. We had no idea of an operation until you told us. I am so glad the doctors think your instrument will be successful and only hope they will try it soon, so that I can have my husband back.[5]

Mabel was growing weary having her husband away from their Boston home for such a protracted period, especially now as she entered the last trimester of her pregnancy. She also kept the truth from him about what people were saying: "While he is working, the papers are laughing at him and classing him with the crowd of refrigerator men and nostrum inventors," Mabel wrote to her mother.

Now that everyone knew he was trying to create an invention to help the president, the newspapers were just waiting for him to fail. Just like Orton and Gray had. Mabel, though, was smart enough to separate her emotions from the greater picture.

Mabel was tired of the press doubting her husband and ridiculing him. For she knew that her husband valued human life above all else. He wanted to make people's lives better, the way he had done with her and so many fortunate others. The way he had done with the telephone. Bell would work until he succeeded, or dropped, whichever came first.

> Poor Mrs. Garfield, how sorry I am for her. She must be a pretty brave woman to keep up her courage. According to one paper, the whole nation leans upon her courage. I hope that the worst is over, but long for news.

So did Bell. If Dr. Bliss would just summon him, he felt he could do a great service to the president and the nation. His invention worked, he knew it did. He could save the president's life. As always, Mabel brilliantly distracted her husband with news of his family.

> Daisy's picture was not very successful Friday, so she tries again today. She is just now trotting around the room full of life and mischief unable to keep still a moment.

Daisy was the baby in the family, already two and a half, her father realized. Even in the month he had been away from home, he knew his daughter had changed as any child would at that age.

> Elsie talks about poor Mr. Garfield and wants to kick bad man that hurt him. I tell her Papa has gone to make poor Mr. Garfield well, but she wants to kick bad man.

Elsie was Bell's oldest daughter, all of four years old. Her childhood had been interrupted by the terrible spectacle of an attempted presidential assassination. Elsie was fully cognizant that he was intervening to save the president's life. It was the kind of pressure that only Robert Lincoln could understand.

> It continues cool but rather damp here. We did have a scare the other day. Mrs. Gilbert's boy had what looked like diphtheria, however I think it is a false alarm, the child is well and bright today, but of course my children are kept far away and are very well and Dr. Putnam says there is no danger, if they are kept away.

Known as "the strangling angel of children," diphtheria was a leading cause of childhood death. A virulent bacterium entered the body through mouth or skin, resulting in fever, hoarseness, and barking. In the worst cases, the sac around the heart swelled, causing death. While doctors like Putnam, the Bell family physician, didn't know what to do about it, the bacteria itself had been isolated by scientists. But there was no known cure or vaccine.

I send a cheque and some cards though I almost hope they may come too late. My love, I love you very much and my thoughts are constantly with you.

Yours ever lovingly, Mabel, Elsie..........Daisy[6]

Before he could take pen in hand to reply, Tainter ran over from the lab with a note that had just arrived from the Executive Mansion. Bell tore it open. It was what he had been anxiously awaiting. As he read, he saw that Dr. Bliss was requesting him to be at the Executive Mansion late that afternoon.

"The experiment would be made at six o'clock on the person of the President," Bliss wrote to Bell.

"Move the President to a bed without metal box springs," he wrote back to Bliss.[7]

Bell had been specific, because he didn't want to worry about the metal box springs interfering with the induction balance locating the bullet in the president's body. By putting the doctor on the alert now, Bell was certain Bliss would listen.

21

"She Excites in Me the Fire of Lawless Passion"

Whether Alexander Graham Bell succeeded or not, it would be amid the glare of the spotlight. Reporters from the nation's major papers—the *New York Times, Washington Post, San Francisco Chronicle,* and *St. Louis Post-Dispatch*—had gathered in Washington to cover the president's deteriorating condition. If and when President Garfield died, they were ready to go with the story like a pack of jackals.

Bell was determined: that story must *never* be written. He set to work testing new ideas to further improve his invention. A condenser stores an electrical charge and gives an electrical apparatus a surge of juice when needed. He found that a condenser improved the hearing distance of the instrument.

The idea had occurred to him some days before, but he could not spare the time to make a condenser and did not know where to get one. He looked all over. Eventually, Bell found one in the detritus of his laboratory. He and Tainter attached it to the induction balance. At 4:30 p.m., a hansom cab clattered to the curb in front of the Volta Laboratory.

Bell and Tainter came out with their precious cargo. They carefully placed it in a secure space in the cab. Their hansom bumped over the Washington cobblestones, heading down Pennsylvania Avenue to the Executive Mansion. Entering the president's sick room upstairs, Bell saw the president propped up with many pillows.

As Bell came abreast, he noticed Garfield's sallow complexion. Previously, when Bell had seen him, he had had the look of a man who indulged in good living, and who was accustomed to working in the open air. Now, there was none of that. The president of the United States of America lay upon his back with his head turned toward a white screen that could provide privacy when employed.

His eyes were closed and a calm peaceful expression came upon his countenance. The president was enjoying a few blessed moments of sleep. Garfield had done as he had said he would when he was shot weeks before; he had borne his pain stoically, as he believed the president of the United States should. He never complained when Bliss did his painful probing. And he believed absolutely in his childhood friend's ministrations. He had no doubt that he was getting the best of care.

Looking down on the president's pain-wracked body, if there was any moment in which Bell had a real danger of failing, it was this one. He never thought nor claimed to hold a human life in his hands. Doctors are trained for such moments; inventors are not. Bell quickly realized that if his invention was going to be successful, he had to look at this like any scientific experiment and the president as his subject.

If he thought that the president's life hung in the balance, he would never be able to do his job. He gazed around the room. Bell came to the conclusion that the wires must enter by the open door. But that necessitated lengthening the wires, so as to reach from there across to the surgeon's room into the hall or passage way.

He strung the wires from the induction balance to the telephone receiver in the outside hallway. Then suddenly, Garfield awakened. Bliss hustled over to take charge as Barnes and Woodward changed the president's dressing. Back outside at the telephone receiver, Tainter adjusted the volume, trying to eliminate a persistent and mysterious static.

Bell sent him down to the basement. Maybe there was some metal down there that the induction balance was picking up on; that could account for the persistent static. As Tainter was bounding down the stairs, Bliss came out to tell Bell that it was time to try his invention.

Bliss had been anticipating this moment. He would be the one to wield the exploring coils of the induction balance. Bell was rather surprised at this; for that had not been their agreement. But he acquiesced. Bliss took the exploring coils and went over to the president, as Bell went to listen at the phone.

The surgical screen had been removed and an assistant knelt at the bedside supporting Garfield, who had turned over on his side, resting his head upon the man's shoulder, and helping to support him by clasping the assistant around the neck. Bliss moved the exploring coil from the wound down the back, beside the spine, and near the liver.

For a second time, Bell was surprised. He understood from others that they expected to find the bullet lodged in the wall of the abdomen somewhere in front. Bell had been too busy to see all the news reports. He didn't know that Bliss had stated that the bullet was near the president's liver. But instead of a ringing, which would signify the bullet had been found, there was just the same, persistent static.

Bell was chagrined. He had tried his invention on over thirty Civil War veterans with bullet fragments or some other such shrapnel still left in their bodies. They were an anonymous test group, former Confederate soldiers who, upon being accepted back into the Union, had to lay down their arms and swear a loyalty oath to it.

That oath was as anathema to the South as a boll weevil infestation to a cotton field. But here they were, sixteen years after the war had ended, allowing the inventor to use them as test subjects in order to save the president of the United States. Their assistance would be for naught, Bell knew, unless he could get his invention to work when it counted.

Each time during the trials, the machine had unfailingly picked out the location of the metal inside the subject. Careful note was taken when the exploring coils came over the entry wound. Sometimes, the bell didn't go off right over the wound; sometimes it went off a few inches away. Medical records were cross-checked with the induction balance's results.

But all Bell heard now when Bliss examined the president with the induction balance was that static. His inventor's mind went to work on how to solve the problem. If the machine worked, and he had no doubt it did, they why didn't it work on President Garfield? There had to be a reason. Before he could figure it out, Bliss, the coils still in his hands, looked up at Bell and shook his head. The examination was over.

Bell had never felt more mortified. He had failed! As he left, he looked back at the figure of the president, being lowered to a more comfortable position on his bed. Once the press found out about the failed attempt, his invention would suffer. He really thought he had contributed something valuable in saving human lives.[1]

Bell's mind kept going back to the just-completed experiment. What was that strange static and why had Dr. Bliss turned the induction balance *away* from the expected bullet site? In trials, the induction balance had detected the position of the lead inside the body every single time. Except for President Garfield. Why was it different with him?

The next day, with the strength and gumption that had seen him charge through Confederate lines under fire, despite the odds against him, Garfield seized a pen with the same tenacity he had once held the reins of the horse that had collapsed under him from the Confederate balls.

July 27, 1881

Dear Mother

Don't be disturbed by conflicting reports about my condition. It is true I am still weak and on my back but I am gaining every day and need only time and patience to bring me through. Give my love to all the relatives and friends and especially to Hetty and Mary.[2]

Your living son,
James A. Garfield

Eliza Ballou Garfield had beaten all the odds. She was eighty years old, at a time when the average life expectancy was forty-nine years.[3] Her son, born into poverty in a log cabin, had become president of the United States. But now, once again, she had to worry about him from afar.

For Crete Garfield, the challenge was much, much greater. Crete and James had had a very difficult marriage.

In the early years, Garfield was away from Crete, first in physical combat on the battlefield and then in verbal combat on Capitol Hill. Crete later said he was home maybe six weeks in the first six years of marriage. Crete also didn't like her mother-in-law very much. Eliza Ballou intervened when she shouldn't. She was very demanding and dominating.[4]

But what really galled Crete was Garfield's lack of passion toward her on his return from his travels; that was unacceptable. Never mind that she was a self-admitted dispassionate woman who did not often display affection, and perhaps her husband was just reacting in kind. Crete was riled, and told her husband of the frustration and anger she felt toward him.

Garfield listened. His conscience, which was already bothering him, could stand it no longer. He broke down and told Crete about Lucia Calhoun, a young, attractive reporter for the *New York Times*. He had met her when she had interviewed him in New York City, which was one of the reasons he'd enjoyed the city so much.

"She excites in me the fire of lawless passion," Garfield admitted to his wife.[5]

"You shall not commit adultery." That was the seventh commandment Moses brought down from Mount Sinai. Garfield had violated it. But like her husband, Crete was a member of the Disciples of Christ. She knew her Bible and she knew Jesus Christ's teachings well.

"For if you forgive men when they sin against you, your heavenly Father will also forgive you. But if you do not forgive men their sins, your Father will not forgive your sins," Jesus said in Matthew 6:14-1.

Crete chose to follow Jesus's path. She forgave her husband his transgression. He knew he was fortunate. Garfield committed like never before to making their marriage work. When the opportunity had come up, Crete hadn't wanted her husband to become president. But when it looked like he might get the nomination, she relented, slightly.

Crete Garfield hoped that when he was nominated, he would be the party's clear choice and not the compromise candidate. She was scrubbing a floor in their Ohio house, when someone gave her the news that Garfield had been nominated for president by the Republicans, on the thirty-sixth ballot. That had not worked out the way she would have liked.

Wives didn't do anything when their husbands ran for president, except to look supportive and demure for Mathew Brady's camera and the artists who worked for *Frank Leslie's Illustrated*. But after the election was a different story. Crete not only supported James, she became his secret agent. The fact that Lucia Calhoun was in New York might also have entered into her decision to help her husband.

On the president elect's orders, the First Lady–elect traveled to New York City incognito, under a phony name, Mrs. Greenfield. She was there to meet with the Stalwarts, one of the New York Republican factions. Crete discussed cabinet suggestions with Roscoe Conkling, the Stalwart leader. But she didn't like or trust him. The married Conkling had had a very public affair.

Understandably, Crete disapproved of men who cheated on their wives. Garfield didn't need to surround himself with men like that. If they could not be entrusted with matters of the heart and morality, if they readily broke the Commandments, how could they be entrusted with matters of the state?

While in New York City, Crete spoke with other politicians. She advised them to name James G. Blaine to the president's cabinet. He had fathered a child out of wedlock, and then married the woman. Blaine was an upstanding man. The politicians clearly listened, and so did her husband, though Garfield was already sold.

Blaine from Maine, and Garfield from Ohio, had formed a bond in the thirteen years they served together as representatives in Congress. Garfield had no problem in naming his old friend as secretary of state. He'd make a good one.

Crete Garfield was not the most social sort, but when she got back to the White House from New York City, she decided to have an open reception in April, one that the public could attend. One of the attendees was Charles Guiteau.

22

"Feeding per Rectum"

Charles Guiteau found Crete Garfield to be "chatty and comfortable." A few days later, a malaria-carrying mosquito from the White House swamp bit Crete; she got the disease. While recovering in the White House, Crete realized how much she loved James, and he, in turn, realized how much he loved her. When Crete was feeling a bit better, Garfield decided that the shore air at their Elberon, New Jersey, home would hasten her recovery. He escorted her to the train depot. Shadowing his every move was Charles Guiteau.

The little man with the equalizer in his pocket was ready to kill Garfield for denying him patronage. But when Guiteau saw how weak and thin Crete was, he decided to spare her the horror of witnessing her husband being shot. Of course, that didn't stop him completely. Guiteau eventually shot her husband. Now Crete was being asked to hold it together in the same way Mary Lincoln had.

Unfortunately, Mary hadn't done so well after her husband's death. Already with deep emotional problems, her husband's assassination sent Mary into a tailspin. That led Robert finally to commit her to a sanitarium. However, this time the situation was decidedly different. Crete Garfield was a stable person. More importantly, James had survived the assassin's bullet. Lincoln hadn't.

Crete had to take care of her children, her home, the duties of First Lady, and most importantly, her severely wounded husband. Speculation swirled around Washington that Eliza Ballou might soon return, to help raise her grandchildren and substitute for Crete at formal functions and receptions.

Crete wasn't raised to voice profanity. Her response to such speculation might best be described by the phrase, "over my dead body," were it not inappropriate under the circumstances.

• • •

Mabel Bell wrote to Alec in late July of 1881.

Friday, July 29, 1881

My dear Alec:

You poor boy, how sorry I am for you in your disappointment. I can imagine just how chagrined and mortified you must have felt when those horrid noises prevented you being sure what you heard.

Never mind, courage; from failure comes success, be worthy of your patient and don't lose heart even if all else are discouraged. I have not the least doubt but that you will eventually succeed. You have never yet failed and will not now. Only I wish I could be with you to help and try and cheer you.

If it were not for the little ones I would come right down. I am only impatient to be with you again and am not the least disturbed about your success. All I dread is that the doctors may be discouraged or lose faith, still I think all will be well if you do not despair. Only it was rather hard on me to raise my hopes so high and then to shatter them for the benefit of telegraph employees.

While Bell's telegraphic ruse had worked, Mabel didn't like it that she had been kept in the dark that way. Bell didn't have a choice. Mabel, though, was very appreciative that he told her all about what it was like to be in the room with the president. He had even drawn a map of the room, with everyone's position, and sent it to her with his previous letter.

I almost feel as if I had been there too. I am so glad you admired the President so much. Don't you think he will live? I wish you had seen Mrs. Garfield too, she must be so noble and womanly brave to keep up through everything as she has done. Dear love, goodbye and keep up your courage and do take care of yourself.

I don't want you to be sick too. I'm afraid we neither of us would be the examples Mr. and Mrs. Garfield are!!

Lovingly—Mabel[1]

Putting the responsibility on himself, Bell was convinced the experiment had failed because the condenser he had put on at the last minute was not properly connected. He and Tainter took the condenser out of the machine and reconnected it, making certain it was properly connected.

Then Bell went out to Armory Square Hospital, Bliss's old home ground. There he found three Civil War veterans who still had lead in their bodies from battle. He passed his magic wand over their bodies. Each time, the bell rang when the bullets were detected. The induction balance worked on all three. The results were perfect!

"I therefore dispatched Mr. Tainter to the Executive Mansion on Sunday morning, July 31st, with a note for Dr. Bliss, to let him know that the instrument was in a condition to be used should any necessity arise for an immediate experiment," Alec later wrote to Mabel.

Desperate to do something lest the president die and be blamed for it Bliss acquiesced.

"We are to try the President tomorrow morning at 8 o'clock. No need for further secrecy," Alec wrote Mabel in a telegram on July 31. The next morning, as he and Tainter were getting ready to go, up in Boston, Mabel sat down to write him another letter.

August 1, 1881

My dear Alec:

I am so glad to hear that you are improving your apparatus. I hope that the second attempt will be successful. I know you deserve it and poor Mr. Garfield must wish you would. I have been looking over the old papers of the first few days of Garfield's illness and wonder how he lived through them, there seems to have been so much confusion and everybody who liked had admittance to him.

At one time, it seems that the whole cabinet called upon him and all their wives were his nurses. I should think all the crowd would literally have worried him to his death. I have never been very ill in my recollection, yet I know how the presence of strangers has fatigued me when I have been sick and how I have felt as if a little more would drive me into a fever.

My heart and mind are constantly occupied with you and the wish for Mr. President's recovery and I long to have you near to tell me all about it. Poor boy, no wonder you are exhausted and headachey. I only hope it won't make your nervous trouble worse. Do take care for my sake my own love. I am quite expecting you home this week.

Lovingly, Your own Mabel[2]

As Mabel was finishing up her letter that morning, Bell and Tainter went back to the White House for the second attempt to locate the bullet in the president's body. Bell described his efforts: "With the view of eliminating any error of observation caused by the pulsations due to simply the movement of the instrument, I lifted the latter to a height about 50 percent above the body of the President and moved it to and fro. It seemed reasonably certain that the area of sound I heard was due to some external cause and was not simply an effort of expectancy."[3]

What could that external cause be? In other experiments he had made the sound was specific. Why had it not been so here? Bell didn't give up. Back at the Volta Laboratory, Bell got a revolver. He took it and the induction balance to a nearby butcher's shop.

"Do you have a side of beef?" he asked the butcher behind the counter.

He told him what he intended to do. Bell's renown must have helped, because the butcher let him try his experiment in his shop. Bell aimed and fired a bullet into a side of beef, then passed

"FEEDING PER RECTUM"

the induction balance over it. The bell rang loudly. His invention had found the bullet easily.

Bell now knew for certain it had to be some outside source at the White House that had caused his experiment to go awry. He determined to get to the bottom of the mystery. With the same determination he had shown in fighting the Boston Fire, "[I] proceeded to the Executive Mansion next morning [August 2] to ascertain from the surgeons whether they were perfectly sure that all metal had been removed from the neighborhood of the bed. It was then recollected that underneath the horsehair mattress on which the president lay was another composed of steel wire."

The steel wire had been causing the static during both attempts. Garfield had been lying on a metal box spring. But before the first attempt was ever even made, Bell had written to Bliss, "Move the President to a bed without metal box springs." Why, then, had Bliss not done as the great inventor had asked?

Bliss never answered that question, nor did he give Bell another opportunity to try the induction balance a third time on the president. Now that Bell had "failed" with his invention, Bliss was determined to succeed with his. While Bell left to visit his very pregnant wife in Boston, it was time for Bliss to step into the spotlight. But he had something to do first.

He let reporters know that Alexander Graham Bell had failed with his invention. The newspapers coast-to-coast excoriated Bell as a charlatan.[4] No one knew what Bliss had done to sabotage both of Bell's attempts to use the induction balance on the president.

Bell kept his questions to himself. For now. It was time to go to Mabel. With Bell's departure, Bliss then felt comfortable coming forward with his invention. Since the president had a poor appetite and needed his nourishment, Bliss had an idea. He would pump food up the president's anus.

"Feeding per rectum. I prefer this expression to those commonly in use as rectal alimentation, not only because it is more terse, but also because it more exactly describes what occurs," he later wrote.

Bliss described it as an "artificial method of sustaining life. Nutrient enemata goes back to the ancient Egyptians, many hundred years before Christ, for which it appears that they had a custom of using emetics and clysters three days in each month to preserve health."[5] However, medicine had progressed considerably since the ancient Egyptians.

More than two decades before Bliss and his family got to Michigan, in the 1820s, army physician Dr. William Beaumont was stationed on Mackinac Island. Located near Michigan's northern peninsula, it was on Mackinac that Beaumont met Alexis St. Martin, a nineteen-year-old French Canadian trapper. He'd taken a shotgun blast in his stomach, at point-blank range.

St. Martin was lucky just to be alive. Beaumont's examination showed extensive damage. Muscle had been blown to bits. His stomach was perforated from the grapeshot. Ribs were broken due to the force of the blast. Despite the odds of dying due to the blast, let alone blood poisoning, St. Martin survived. Unfortunately for St. Martin, he didn't heal fully.

What was left was a gastric fistula—a permanent hole directly into his stomach, from the outside skin, and which would never heal. Beaumont decided to take advantage of the opportunity of learning about the process of digestion. How did it work? No one really knew much about it.

The answers would take eight years and 238 experiments, conducted at four different army posts to which Beaumont was billeted. St. Martin helped for the sake of science. Beaumont's methodology was to tie different kinds of foods to strings. He then inserted them though St. Martin's fistula, directly into his stomach. There was no pain involved.

After a while, Beaumont would then take out the string and examine what the gastric juice had done to the food. He also removed a small quantity of gastric juice. In this way, through careful observation and notation, Beaumont documented the process of digestion. He proved that food was digested in the stomach and no other place in the human body.

Subsequently hailed as the father of gastric physiology, Beaumont wrote up his work in the seminal book, *Experiments and Observations on the Gastric Juice and the Physiology of Digestion*, published in 1833. Beaumont's book became a medical staple. So when D. W. Bliss proposed to feed the president through the rectum, he had to know it wouldn't work.[6]

What it was, was torture.

23

"We Were Enabled . . . to Use Specially Prepared Blood"

"Probably the earliest form of syringe was that used by the Egyptians, consisting of a pipe with a bladder tied upon one end," Bliss wrote in his sixteen-page book of 1882, *Feeding Per Rectum: As Illustrated in the Case of the Late President Garfield, and Others.* "From these primitive means resulted our present system, by which a continuous stream may be thrown to almost any point in the large intestine. All are acquainted with the so-called 'fountain' syringe, by which a continual drench of the lower bowel may be prolonged at pleasure."

Pleasure? As it turned out Bliss soon admitted to having tortured before, another patient he had "fed" through the rectum: "In one instance (that of a distinguished Senator, now dead), I was obliged to frequently introduce the tube of the stomach pump very nearly the whole length of the transverse colon."

Bliss did this without anesthetic, tearing up the senator's lower intestine with his invasive tube. He doesn't write how he died. Regarding the composition of the enemata, Bliss quoted a German doctor—a "Dr. Kaufmann (Deutsche Zeitsch. farprakt. Med., No. 44, 1877)"—who had conducted such torture on his patients: "It is essential that the pancreatic gland which is to be used, be from an animal quite recently killed, as the tissues and juice of that gland lose their property very quickly if the temperature of the surrounding air is at all high. It is well to take away the fat and cellular (connective) tissue, and inject only the meat and glandular tissue, very finely divided and thoroughly mixed."

Bliss then discussed the so-called medical use of defibrinated blood, injected up the rectum, noting that other doctors did so, "but there seems to have been a general experience of difficulty arising from the strong tendency of blood to decompose in the rectum." That didn't stop Bliss. "In the case of President Garfield we were enabled, through the kindness of Dr. Smith, to use specially prepared blood."

By using blood that had been specifically prepared for this purpose, the idea was that the body would automatically absorb the blood's nutrients, thus feeding the patient. Despite the fact that the vast majority of the medical profession thought this treatment nonsense, Bliss injected defibrinated blood up Garfield's rectum and into his intestines. He dutifully reported the results, though without detail or measurements: "It was found, however, that the same trouble arose as in the last case cited, and we were forced to discontinue it. Whether this result was due to the general debility of the patient or to the unstable nature of the substance used, I cannot say, but it is probably that both causes contributed."

How did Garfield respond to having blood injected up his rectum? Bliss didn't keep any records, and Garfield never spoke of it, except perhaps privately to Crete. But now that Garfield hadn't taken to having blood injected up his rectum, it was time to try food instead.

"The question is often asked, 'How long can life be supported by rectal feeding?' Experience teaches that, except in cases of malignant disease (always self-limited), there is practically no limit," Bliss wrote, though exactly who was asking that question is unclear.

Bliss then had the unique opportunity to humiliate someone who had humiliated him. It was Surgeon General Barnes who had put the Nelaton probe into Lincoln's brain, while Bliss was forced to watch. So Bliss made Barnes into an errand boy. He dispatched Barnes to his own dispensary. There, he delivered a formula to W. F. Cursor, his assistant apothecary.

"Make this up quickly," said the Surgeon General.

Cursor looked down at the formula. It wasn't exactly the medications one would expect to treat the wounded president.

Beef Extract.—Directions.—Infuse a third of a pound of fresh beef, finely minced, in 14 ounces of cold soft water, to which a few drops (4 or 5) of muriatic acid and a little salt (from 10 to 18 grains) have been added. After digesting for an hour to an hour and a quarter, strain it through a sieve and wash the residue with 5 ounces of cold water, pressing it to remove all soluble matter. The mixed liquid will contain the whole of the soluble constituents of the meat.

The temperature should not be raised above 100° F., as at the temperature of 113° F., a considerable portion of the albumen, a very important constituent, will be coagulated.

Once the beef extract was made, the apothecary was to take two ounces of the mixture and add to it, "2 drachms [one eighth of a fluid ounce] of Beef Peptonoids, and 5 drachms whiskey." When it was all mixed up, Barnes had it delivered to the White House. Now it was time to do it.

Bliss's great invention was the same as the Egyptians had used two thousand years earlier—tubing inserted, without anesthetic, up the rectum. Garfield winced at the pain of his body being invaded yet again. On the far end of the tube was the bladder, in which reposed the feeding mixture the government apothecary had made up for the occasion.

As Garfield waited, he suddenly felt the coldness of the mixture shooting into his intestines, and the pain, and the sensation of needing to urinate immediately.

As Bliss later described it in his book: "Occasionally 5 to 10 drops of deodorized tinct. opii [tincture of opium] were added as an additional nerve stimulant and anodyne, and also to secure retention of the enema."

And then, to vary things a little, Bliss tried innovating his mixture. "For the first five or six days, the yolk of an egg was added to the injections, but [it] was the cause of annoying and offensive flatus. This symptom was promptly relieved by discontinuing the egg, and temporarily adding about a drachm of willow charcoal."

Despite these temporary setbacks, Bliss claimed that since the president had lost his appetite, he was *only* fed through his rectum. And he had physical proof: "Once in twenty-four hours a discharge of healthy feces occurred, generally of such consistence and form, as would justify the belief that digestion had taken place in the small intestines."[1]

Bliss was lying. Not about the feces, but the food.

Dr. William Beaumont had already proven that digestion only took place in the stomach, and at no other place in the body. Everything that went up Garfield's intestine came right out the same way. But to have feces meant that food was digested. Bliss's claim that the president took no food by mouth is therefore patently false.

Since the bullet had not yet been found, it was time to operate again. Bliss later explained his procedure to the *New York Times*.

We passed a flexible catheter through the opening previously made which readily coursed through the crest of the illus, a distance of about seven inches. This captivity had been evacuated twice daily by passing through the cavity, previously inserted in the wound track, an aqueous solution of pomegranate potash from a small hand fountain, slightly elevated, the water and pus returning and escaping at the opening externally.

We extended the incision previously made downward and forward through the skin, through the internal and extremal oblique muscles of the abdomen, into the pus channel. Upon carrying a long curved director through the opening between the fractured rib downward to the point of incision, there was a deeper channel which had not been exposed by the operation thus far. The incision was carried through into the deeper track, exposing the end of the director. A catheter was then passed into a portion of the track below the incision a distance of three and one half inches.[2]

After this operation, Garfield began a slow decline. Blood poisoning ravaged his body. Even as Bliss continued to put the best face on it, issuing positive health bulletins for the nation and the world, those on the inside knew that the president had little or no hope of survival.

On August 17, forty-seven days after Garfield had been shot—Guiteau was still languishing in Capitol Prison—Lucretia Garfield received a telegram addressed specifically to her.

> To Mrs. Garfield, Washington, D.C.
>
> I am most anxious to know how the President is to-day, and to express my deep sympathy with you both.
>
> *The Queen, Osborne*

Lucretia replied quickly.

> Her Majesty, Queen Victoria, Osborne, England
>
> Your Majesty's kind inquiry finds the president's condition changed for the better. In the judgment of his medical advisers, there is strong hope of his recovery. His mind is entirely clear and your majesty's kind expression of sympathy is most grateful to him, as they are gratefully acknowledged by me.
>
> *Lucretia R. Garfield*[3]

What was she supposed to write? That her husband was dying and his vice president, Chester A. Arthur, was an incompetent who would soon take over? Oh, that would be guaranteed to instill confidence in the American government! No, Crete knew what her role was as First Lady, but more importantly, she knew what her role was to her husband. And that was to take care of him.

As August gave way to September, Garfield watched and felt as his once strong, vital body continued its decline. He was in constant pain and knew that the end of his life was drawing near, yet he still comported himself as he felt a president should, with dignity and humility. He never once complained to Crete, who stayed by his side constantly, nor did he ask for anything special.

Up in Boston, Mabel seemed to be all right, so Bell didn't stay long.

He got things in order for a nurse, hugged and kissed his kids. What James Garfield didn't know was that Bell was as dedicated to him as Major David G. Swaim.

Swaim was the Judge Advocate General. Coincidentally, the initials of his office were also those of "James Abram Garfield." Swaim was an old army friend of Garfield's. They had become best buddies under fire. The president liked to have Swaim around to relax with over a game of cards or billiards.[4]

Back to Manhattan on the train, then across the Hudson to New Jersey, the train south from Jersey City to DC, and then Bell was back in his lab. Bell and Tainter worked feverishly on further perfecting the induction balance. When he used it this third time on the president, he would not allow Dr. Bliss to destroy his experiment.

This time, he would make sure that all the metal had been removed, including the box spring. What Bell didn't know was that there was not going to be a "next time." This time, he was up against a person who had had experience manipulating the press. Where Elisha Gray and others had not been able to marshal press support for their outrageous charges that they had invented the telephone first—thus discrediting Bell—Bliss was a lot smarter.

After Bell's last attempt, Bliss had told the press a selective version of the truth—both Bell and his invention had failed. The press bought it and discredited both in their stories. There was going to be no third attempt because, this time, there was no pressure on Bliss to bring Bell back; he had seen to that by deliberately sabotaging the first two attempts.

While hopelessly waiting for his next summons to the White House that never came, Bell received a letter from Mabel. In it, she said that on August 15, she had given birth to a boy, prematurely. "[He was] a strong and healthy little fellow [and] might have pulled through if they could have once established regular breathing," Mabel later wrote.

Their infant son had survived six hours and then died. The Bells were given a task no parent should ever have: they had to name their dead child before they buried him. They named him Edward, and Bell studiously sent in his birth announcement to the *London Times*. His son was certainly entitled to that recognition.

Bell knew the childhood mortality rate, just as President Lincoln had. In Massachusetts, it was 15 percent.[5] But Bell might be able to do something about it. He plunged into his work: he had a new idea for a machine to assist with breathing. Bell channeled his grief into experiments to create what he called the "vacuum jacket," the world's first artificial respirator.[6]

24

"Mr. President . . . You Are Getting Out of the Woods"

As Bell worked at perfecting his newest invention, across town at the White House, James and Crete Garfield were making plans of their own. Tired of Bliss's constant invasion of his body, Garfield wanted a respite. He and Crete made the decision to go to the Jersey Shore in Elberon.

"The President's condition being favorable for such a journey, he is going to be moved to his home in Long Branch New Jersey to continue his convalescence," Bliss put out in a new bulletin.

It only took one day to make the necessary arrangements for the journey. The special train that had carried Crete to the White House from New Jersey would now reverse direction. Trunks and boxes were packed for deployment the following day.

On September 6, all was in readiness. At a few minutes past 5:00 a.m., several carriages and an Adams Express Wagon, stood on the drive near the White House's main entrance. The large wagon was covered and furnished with side and end curtains. It was near 6:00 a.m., when quite a commotion became apparent in the Executive Mansion. A little caravan came out.

There was Crete, Bliss, Colonel Rockwell, and Major Swaim. This tight party with its precious cargo proceeded slowly out the gates of the White House and toward the train station. Garfield was on a stretcher, which the bearers carefully carried to the waiting express wagon. Once his passenger was safely ensconced, the wagon driver urged his horses on into a lively walk.

Walking on either side of the wagon were three members of the Metropolitan Police, whose purpose was to keep the street clear. When the procession arrived at the Baltimore and Potomac, the express wagon was given immediate access to the train shed, while the others were forced to board the train through the lobby.

The attendants quickly removed the president on his stretcher. Accompanied by Crete, they took him into a special car that had been fitted out for the occasion with a special, heavily padded mattress that Bliss had approved. He might have missed the irony.

With a jerk, the train pulled out of the station, rolling out of the depot. But just a few minutes later, inside his car, Garfield felt the train slowing up. He heard the brakes engage with a loud "rrrrrr" and suddenly, they stopped.

"What does this mean?" Garfield asked.

Colonel Rockwell looked out the window and saw what was happening—an approaching train was being moved out of the way onto a siding. Robert Lincoln had put the word out to remove everything on the tracks in front of the president's train, so he could have a safe, fast ride to the Jersey Shore.

"Only a momentary detention," Colonel Rockwell then replied.

"But important events are ofttimes the result of the moment," Garfield reposted.

He was feeling pretty good. For the moment. He was going to see and smell the ocean.

After a trip of two hundred and thirty-three miles, the president's train arrived in Elberon seven hours later. The train sped through towns at an average speed of 33.5 miles per hour, with Americans crowding the tracks to gaze mournfully. Maybe God could help *this* president survive.[1]

September 1881

Elberon is located on the Atlantic coast of New Jersey. Mary Lincoln had visited the place at the suggestion of her family physician in 1861. The town received national publicity from her visit. That and President Grant's buying a summer home there in 1869 had led to the place becoming a resort destination for people with money, like Edwin Booth, also a frequent visitor.

Garfield had been visiting Crete while she was recovering from malaria there in June. They stayed together for a few days at the Elberon Hotel. Grant happened to be staying the night in his son Fred's house across the street. When he found out that Garfield, the man who had beaten him, was in the hotel, he got angry.

When he came into the dining room where the Garfields were having dinner at the Elberon Hotel, Grant completely ignored them. He showed the president of the United States and his First Lady less respect than he had Robert E. Lee at Wilmer McLean's home at Appomattox. But he eventually changed his tune.

At a reception held for the president a short time later in Elberon, Grant attended, and he figuratively tipped his hat to Garfield by deigning to speak with him. Garfield kept his usual scholarly perspective. He looked at Grant's presence as a "tardy recognition of the respect due to the office he once held."[2]

Now Garfield was back in Elberon, with more on his mind than Grant's slights.

Arriving at the Elberon train station, he was immediately driven to Francklyn Cottage. When he got to his room, one of the first things that told him he was not in the White House was the odor. Instead of sewage, he smelled the beautiful bouquet of flowers. As he looked around the room, he saw that the place had been "elegantly prepared for his occupancy, and it was made pleasant with many beautiful bouquets and rare plants sent from personal friends.[3]

During the next few weeks, throughout the United States, in Japan, Britain, Romania, and every country in the world, prayers were being offered by millions of people in their homes and places of business for the restoration of the president of the United States. Garfield was the subject of their supplications at the throne of the Almighty. In New York City, things were no different.

At the Thirteenth Street Presbyterian Church, a prayer vigil was held for the president. At the grand cathedral, with Christians of all denominations and with many Jews also in attendance, the president's pastor, Frederick D. Power, addressed the congregation.

His life is before the world, a living epistle, to be known and read of all men. To you I may say, he has had the ever present Comforter, dwelling in the presence of the Holy Spirit during all of these weary days and nights of suffering. He remembers the Lord's day when it comes. On Sunday morning last, I was with him in the White House as he opened his eyes to the holy light. He said, "This [is] the Lord's day; I have reverence for it."

Power paused before the assembled throng before continuing.

Of his own peril of death, he has been mindful and over and over again has said, "I must be prepared for either." This has been the principle of his life, ruling in all his experience, as he explained it to me. "When I meet the duties of each day, as best I can I cheerfully await whatever result may come."

Garfield continued to fight. On the morning of September 9, D. W. Bliss was chatting it up with a newspaper correspondent.

"Doctor, you seem to be feeling pretty well this morning?"

"I should think I was," Bliss answered brightly. "Why, the man is convalescent. His pulse is now down to ninety-six."

Soon Bliss had a talk with his "old friend."

"Mr. President, you are convalescent; you are getting out of the woods."[4]

Nothing could have been further from the truth.

On September 19, Garfield awoke and could see the ocean from his bed, through the windows. As it had arisen at Chickamauga on the second day, the sun was a bloody red disk as it made its appearance. Perhaps Garfield remembered what he had told the Widow Glenn.

"It will indeed be a day of blood."

What had happened to her and her children? The sun continued to rise over the placid water. As it made its pass through the sky of another day, Garfield dozed on and off. At 10:00 p.m., he awoke suddenly from a nap, in a cold sweat. He saw Colonel Rockwell and his old friend Major Swaim by his bed, along with Daniel, a "colored" attendant.

"Oh Swaim, this terrible pain," Garfield yelled out, placing his hand over his heart.

"Is there anything I can do for you?" Swaim asked.

"Some water."

Striding quickly to the other side of the room, Swaim poured an ounce and a half of Poland water into a glass, handing it to Garfield. The president had the strength to grip the glass. Swaim raised his head up to help him drink the water "very naturally."

Handing the glass to Daniel, Swaim took a napkin and wiped Garfield's forehead free of sweat.

"Oh, Swaim, this terrible pain. Oh, Swaim."

Obligingly, Swaim put his hand on Garfield's chest. The skin was tender. At the touch of his friend's hands, Garfield's hands went up reflexively, as if in defense of a blow from an enemy.

"Oh, Swaim, can't you stop this?"[5] Garfield pleaded.

He stared up at Swaim with a fixed gaze, his dark eyes as intense as when he was charging through the woods, trying to reach Thomas with word to hold the line.

"Are you suffering much pain?" Swaim asked.

When Garfield didn't answer, he asked the question again. This time, when he got no response, he shouted over to Daniel.

"Get Mrs. Garfield and Dr. Bliss!"

Daniel ran into the room next door, where Bliss was taking a break.

"General Swaim wants you quick!"

Daniel ran back with Bliss at his heels. It was dark. Thomas Alva Edison's electric lamp had been patented only nineteen months earlier. Until the White House was wired, Daniel would do what he did now, taking the candle from behind the screen near the door. He raised it so that the light fell full upon Garfield's face.

Bliss observed "the pallor, the upturned eyes, the gasping respiration, and the total unconsciousness."

"My God, Swaim! The president is dying!"

Bliss turned to Daniel.

"Call Mrs. Garfield immediately!"

On his way to Crete's room, Daniel told Colonel Rockwell what was happening. When Daniel told Crete, she ran out so quickly, she just magically appeared in the sick room, without anyone hearing her approach or seeing her come in.

"Oh! What is the matter?" Crete exclaimed.

"Mrs. Garfield, the president is dying," answered Bliss.

Leaning over her husband, Crete fervently kissed his brow.

"Oh! Why am I made to suffer this cruel wrong?" she exclaimed.

Bliss felt for Garfield's pulse; it was in vain. He put his ear over the region of his patient's heart. Restoratives, which were always at hand, were gotten instantly. Maybe this time it worked, because he heard "[a] faint, fluttering pulsation of the heart, gradually fading to indistinctness."

He put his ear over Garfield's heart once again and heard nothing. By then, Rockwell was also in the room with Crete and Daniel. Bliss later wrote, "At 10:35, I raised my head from the breast of my dead friend and said to the sorrowful group, 'It is over.'"

One by one the men passed out of the room, leaving Crete alone with her husband. Thus she remained for more than an hour, "gazing upon [Garfield's] lifeless features, when Colonel Rockwell, fearing the effect upon her health, touched her arm and begged her to retire, which she did."[6]

25

"The Bullet Was Not in Any Part of the Area Explored!"

In New York City, Vice President Chester A. Arthur was administered the oath of office, becoming the twenty-first president of the United States. Arthur followed Andrew Johnson as the second president to take office after his predecessor was shot. He soon left for New Jersey, to be with the newly widowed Lucretia and to offer his condolences.

Robert Lincoln and the other members of the president's cabinet took the train down from Washington to confer on the arrangement of a program for the funeral of the president. After the conference, a plan for the funeral was given for the public's information.

Elberon, New Jersey, September 20, 1881

The remains of the president of the United States will be removed to Washington by special train on Wednesday, September 21, leaving Elberon at 10 a.m. and arriving in Washington at 4 p.m.

This train was going to take an hour off the ride by going even faster than previously.

Detachments from the United States Army and from the marines of the Navy will be in attendance on arrival to perform escort duty. The remains will lie in state in the rotunda of the capital [sic] on Thursday and Friday. Religious ceremonies will be observed in the rotunda at 3 o'clock on Friday afternoon.

At 5 o'clock, the remains will be transferred to the funeral car and be removed to Cleveland, Ohio, via the Pennsylvania Railroad, arriving there Saturday at 2 p.m. The remains will lie in state in Cleveland until Monday at 2 p.m., and then be interred in Lakeview Cemetery.

Robert Todd Lincoln, Secretary of War

While Robert Lincoln was drafting that bulletin, on the afternoon of Tuesday, September 20, a three-and-a-half-hour autopsy was conducted by Bliss; Dr. D. S. Lamb, assistant surgeon at the Medical Museum of Washington; and Dr. Robert Reyburn. They were effectively functioning as coroners.

There are two things a coroner must do in the case of a homicide. He must determine the manner of death and the cause of death. They are not the same. The manner of death here seemed obvious—gunshot wound. But how did that lead to the president's death?

A gunshot wound could lead to excessive blood loss, which would become the cause of death. Or, the bullet could puncture the heart causing heart stoppage, which would again become the cause of death. The victim could also die later from something else. The important thing is that the coroner should never have a personal stake in the outcome of his investigation.

The coroners found that the bullet fired from Guiteau's gun was the method of death. The doctors removed physical evidence of the bullet wound, to be used against the murderer. The cause of death was noted as blood poisoning resulting from the bullet wound. However, the details of the coroner's autopsy report did not back up their conclusions.

Bell had just written his wife a telegram, with news that their son's birth announcement had run in the *London Times*.[1] Shortly thereafter, he read in the newspaper the specific findings of the autopsy of Garfield's body, in which Bliss had participated, according to the report. It didn't take him long to pick up his pen, get a piece of paper, and write Mabel a letter, correctly interpreting what the coroners had found.

I feel much disturbed by the result of the autopsy of the President. It is now rendered quite certain why it was [*sic*] the result of the experiment with the Induction Balance was "not satisfactory," for the bullet was not in any part of the area explored!

The autopsy showed that Bliss had created a *false* wound track with his painful probing. He had taken a three-inch entry wound and, in probing for the bullet, made a pus-infected wound track, twenty-one inches long. Worse, it was a *false* wound track, leading *away* from the bullet. Further, the report said, Garfield was found to be suffering from extensive blood poisoning.

That was the cause of death. But it was even worse than that.

In their autopsy report, the doctors had mentioned a four-by-six-inch abscess between the liver and the transverse colon that was filled with a "greenish yellow fluid." But modern analysis of the report suggests that the doctors failed to recognize that this condition pointed toward a gallbladder perforation, which could have resulted in cholecystitis and eventual death, if left untreated.[2] It was Bliss's painful probing without anesthesia that had punctured Garfield's bladder.[3]

Bell now knew that Bliss had told the press the bullet was near the president's liver and never deviated from that opinion. But the autopsy showed the bullet on the other side of the body, away from the liver, in the area Bliss *deliberately* did not explore. Rather than taking advantage of Bell's invention to painlessly explore the entire area, Bliss only explored near the liver, where he maintained the bullet had lodged.

As for Bliss, if the bullet were to be found anywhere else, he would lose face and money. Never mind that he would also lose a life. He hoped once again to have his practice benefit from his having treated a president, this time as chief physician, no matter whether his patient survived or died.

Bell's anguish and sadness are apparent as he continues his letter to Mabel.

This is most mortifying to me and I can hardly bear to think of it, for I feel that now the finger of scorn will be pointed at the Induction Balance and at me, and all the hard work I have gone through seems thrown away. I feel all the more mortified because I feel that I have really accomplished a great work and have devised an apparatus that will be of inestimable use in surgery, but this mistake will re-act against its introduction. The patients I am anxious to benefit would hardly be willing to risk an operation, even if the bullets were properly located by the Induction Balance, after what has occurred. I shall look with anxiety for the unsparing denunciations that will doubtless appear shortly in the newspaper and I shall be glad indeed to go with you to Italy or anywhere else.

Then he described what had just happened in Washington.

Poor President Garfield was taken to the Capital today. We all witnessed the procession. Our flag hangs at half-mast out of the nursery window and all the houses here have signs of mourning. I thought it unnecessary to ask you to show some signs of a similar kind in Cambridge.

Write to me darling. I want to hear from you so much. It seems an age since we left.

Your loving husband, Alec.[4]

• • •

John Wilkes Booth had actually been caught alive. He'd been wounded by Boston Corbett, a trigger-happy Union soldier, was paralyzed by the bullet, and died soon after. Booth's pretender, Charles Guiteau, had also been caught alive, but was doing quite well in prison. Three squares a day and medical care. He hadn't lived that well in years.

With the president now dead, it was time to charge Charles Guiteau accordingly. Since he had shot Garfield after thinking out his crime, George Corkhill, the federal attorney for Washington DC, charged him with first-degree murder in Garfield's assassination. There was no special law for killing a president; it carried the same penalty as killing anyone else.

If convicted, Charles Guiteau would be the special guest at his own neck-stretching party. But not if Frances Guiteau had anything to do with it. As she had done before, Guiteau's sister came to her brother's rescue. She knew he was insane, that he was not responsible for his actions. She had seen that with her own eyes, when she avoided becoming his first victim.

Appealing to her husband, attorney George Scoville came to Washington to represent his brother-in-law. The first thing Scoville did was ask presiding judge Walter Cox for a continuance. He needed time to get witnesses together for his defense.

"The defense intends to make two primary arguments, that the defendant was legally insane at the time he shot the president and that President Garfield's death resulted from actions by his doctors malpractice," he told the court.[5]

Cox gave him the time to put together his defense witnesses, during which Guiteau argued with Scoville. For Guiteau, the very thought that people would think him insane was insulting. As for malpractice, George had gotten it wrong. Guiteau wrote out an opening statement he was never allowed to deliver in court: "Three weeks after he [Garfield] was shot, his physicians held a careful examination and officially decided he would recover. Two months after this official announcement he died. Therefore, according to his own physicians, he was not fatally shot. The doctors [doctor] who mistreated him ought to be indicted for murdering James A. Garfield and not me."[6]

The very idea that a doctor could murder a patient in the course of his duties and for his own reasons was so unrealistic no one even considered it. Except for a man who was clinically insane. Charles Guiteau heard voices all right, but he had many moments of lucidity, when he made absolute sense.

Bell watched this drama from afar. He had continued perfecting the induction balance. In a last, desperate attempt to prove its virtue, on October 7, 1881, Bell used it to locate a Confederate ball in the cheek of Calvin E. Pratt of Brooklyn, who had taken the hit in the Battle of Gaines' Mill, June, 1862.[7]

The successful public test of Bell's invention that could revolutionize surgery was largely ignored. Nobody cared, least of all the press. Besides, it could take such news days to go all over the country. Just breaking was a much more sensational story about an attempt on Charles Guiteau's life that was an inside job. Because there had been lynch talk, Guiteau had been moved to a small, impenetrable brick cell. Locked by a thick wooden door, the only opening was at the top, large enough to pass him his food, which meant that a hand could also come through it, holding a gun. That's what happened. A hand snaked through. It fired, and the shot just missed Guiteau.

The erstwhile assassin was prison guard William Mason. Taken into custody and charged, he got donations from supporters to pay for his defense. While Mason was working his problems out, his intended victim went to trial. The little man looked even smaller in the oversized black suit and white shirt he wore for the first day of his trial on November 14, 1881.

The courtroom in the District's old criminal court building was filled to capacity. Since Guiteau had shot the president, he was not exactly popular. It was hard to pick an impartial jury. It took three days to conduct a voir dire of 175 jurors. Two years before, in 1879, the Supreme Court had ruled that a state may constitutionally "confine the selection [of jurors] to males."[8]

Washington DC was no different than the rest of the nation. At the end of the third day, Judge Cox and the lawyers had whittled their numbers down to twelve and two alternates, all men. Once that was done, it was time to begin the trial. The prosecution gave their opening, and Scoville followed. He emphasized "insanity" as his principal defense.

Then the prosecution opened their case with testimony from their witnesses. Blaine testified about seeing Garfield shot down at the depot. Patrick Kearney, the cop who had arrested Guiteau as he attempted to flee the depot after shooting Garfield, also testified.

And then the prosecution's star witness came forward to the stand.

"Do you Doctor Doctor Willard Bliss swear to tell the truth, the whole truth and nothing but the truth, so help you God?" asked the clerk.

26

"I Think the Doctors Did the Work"

D. W. Bliss had his hand on the Bible.

"I do," Bliss answered.

He took his hand off the Bible and took the witness stand. The courtroom was soon hushed; people filled the polished wooden benches and were on the edge of their seats. What would the president's chief physician say?

After establishing Bliss's bona fides for the jury and that he had been the president's surgeon and attending physician, as well as a member of the team that conducted the autopsy, the prosecutor got down to it. People gasped as he produced the portion of Garfield's spine that the doctors had cut out during their autopsy.

Bliss used it to show how the bullet from Guiteau's gun had narrowly missed a vertebrae. The prosecutor then asked what had caused the president's death.

"The wound made by the ball was the immediate occasion of death," Bliss testified.[1]

Some cried as he spoke further about the damage Guiteau's gunshot had done to the president's body. Bliss made it clear during his testimony. It made no difference how long it had taken.[2] Guiteau's shot was what had caused the president's death.

As for Bill Jones, he was not in the courtroom. A farmer, Jones was out getting loaded. Then he got on his horse, all stoked up and angry, and decided it was time to kill the president's assassin with the gun that he carried. When the testimony was completed that day, Guiteau was loaded in shackles into the Metropolitan Police van.

Jones was riding a spirited horse. He followed the prisoner from the court to within a few blocks of the Jail, when he suddenly spurred his horse, darted through the crowd, drew a revolver and fired into the prison van. Guiteau, who was sitting near the door, caught a glimpse of Jones as he drew the weapon and dodged.

The bullet sped over his head and lodged in the side of the wagon. Jones, believing he had killed Guiteau, dug the spurs into his horse's side and escaped arrest at that time. He was captured shortly afterward near Fredericksburg, Va. He was [later] tried and acquitted.[3]

The press referred to him as "Bill Jones, the Avenger."

A few days after he had avoided the bullet from Farmer Jones's gun, Charles Guiteau took the stand in his own defense. Scoville's direct examination took some time. He did not have a cooperative client, which in this case helped considerably.

Guiteau's testimony sounded like the ravings of a lunatic. He testified that killing the president was an act he did for the good of the country, under orders from "Jesus Christ & Company." After Scoville finished his direct examination, retired judge John K. Porter, representing the prosecution, got up to cross-examine the witness.

"Did you pass through the ordeal of the Oneida Community and maintain your virtue?" Porter asked.

It was a Victorian way of asking Guiteau if he had been monogamous.

"Well, not absolutely," Guiteau answered truthfully.

"I thought you said yesterday that you did?"

"I said, and I intended to say, although they misreported me [in the press] that I had been mostly a strictly virtuous man there. They left out the word 'mostly.' That is what I intended to say. As a matter of fact, if you want to know the truth, I had to do [sex] with three distinct women in a very short time. But aside from that, I was strictly virtuous."

Porter had his opening, but declined it. Sex was not something you discussed at length in court or any place else. Instead, he moved on to a discussion of the shooting.

"The only inspiration that you had, as I understand you, was to use a pistol on the president?"

"The inspiration consisted in trying to remove the president for the good of the American people, and all these details are nothing," Guiteau replied.

"Were you inspired to remove him by murder?"

"I was inspired to execute the divine will."

"By murder?" Porter wondered aloud.

"So-called; yes, sir; so-called murder."

"You intended to do it?"

Answering "yes" would be to admit to premeditated, first-degree murder.

"I intended to execute the divine will, sir," Guiteau testified.

"You did not succeed," Porter stated.

"I think the doctors did the work," Guiteau answered.

Guiteau had heard Bliss testify. He was a good lawyer, trying to make the case that Bliss, who had been in charge of the president's treatment, had shown depraved indifference to human life, the legal definition of second-degree murder. It was Dr. Doctor Willard Bliss, Guiteau was claiming, who therefore should be tried for murder. Not he.

"The Deity tried, and you tried, and both failed, but the doctors succeeded?" asked an incredulous Porter.

"The Deity confirmed my act by letting the president down as gently as he did."

"Do you think that it was letting him down gently to allow him to suffer that torture, over which you professed to feel so much solicitude, during those long months?" Porter asked, his ire rising.

Scoville should have been on his feet shouting, "Objection, counsel's comment is prejudicial." Instead he stayed seated and kept his mouth shut.

"The whole matter was in the hands of the Deity, and I do not wish to discuss it any further in this connection," Guiteau continued, without his counsel stopping him as he put his neck further into the noose. "Of course, I appreciate the mere outward fact of the president's disability in his long sickness as much as any person in the world. That is a very narrow view to take of this matter—just the mere outward fact of the president's disability and sickness."[4]

If Scoville had taken Guiteau's doctor argument seriously, he could have then called Alexander Graham Bell to the stand. Bell would have confirmed Guiteau's suspicions about how Bliss's treatment killed the president. Instead, the defense attorney decided to abandon any claim that the doctor(s) had anything to do with the president's death. For the rest of the trial, Scoville used expert witnesses to try to convince the jury that Guiteau was insane when he shot the president.

December 1881

This was a battle for history, not only in the courtroom but also in the public press. How would it play out? Who would ultimately be held responsible for James Garfield's murder? Would Bell's great invention, the induction balance, be accepted by the public as the medical marvel it was, or would it be relegated to a backroom of the Smithsonian?

It all depended upon how the newspapers reported events that historians would later shape into a coherent narrative. Bliss, of course, had a personal stake in the outcome. During the year, his wife Sophia had died, but he didn't pause to grieve.

He had just testified against Guiteau. Before the case was given to the jury, and with the trial still on, Bliss decided to hammer the nails into the little man's coffin. Bliss wrote an article for the December 1881 issue of *Century Magazine*. Once again, Bliss found himself in the right place at the right time.

The successor to *Scribner's Monthly Magazine*, the *Century Magazine* was the news magazine that became the gold standard of journalistic reporting, from that first issue in which Bliss's article appeared until the end of the nineteenth century. Because that was the premiere issue, Bliss had to have been working on it for a while, to make the deadline for December publication.

Most of the article consisted of self-serving statements, such as this one: "The record which I wish to make now is not that of the surgeon so much as that of the man who loved his patient. Knowing as I did his private and public greatness, few can appreciate my feelings on receiving Secretary Lincoln's message which summoned me to the care of the wounded President."

Bliss makes a number of claims in the article that are patently false: "My first acquaintance with the late President was as a lad at Chagrin Falls, Ohio, about the year 1844."

According to Bliss, Garfield would have been only thirteen years old when they met. That didn't happen. Four months before publication of Bliss's article, White House attendant Thomas Francis Pendel had been attending to Garfield while Bliss was in the room. That's when Garfield told Pendel how he had first met Bliss, when he was an *adult* on the road to the Western Eclectic Institute in Hiram.

The *Century Magazine* article concluded: "His calm obedience and cool courage would possibly have secured recovery without scientific aid, had not the injury been fatal from the start."[5]

This was the only mention of "science" in the article. As for Bell, it was as though he had never existed or tried to save the president's life. The induction balance had already been discredited by the press, just as they had ridiculed Bell's failed efforts. The doctor who had treated the president did not talk about Bell and his invention, because they had "failed." They were irrelevant to the discussion of how the president had died.

It was a story to which every member of the Guiteau jury had access, and was, in fact, prejudicial.

January 13, 1882

If the jury had believed that Guiteau was "not guilty" by reason of insanity, the judge would have sentenced Guiteau to a lunatic asylum for life, instead of death by hanging. But the prosecution had lined up their experts to prove the opposite. The experts had in fact testified to Guiteau's insanity when he shot the president. But then it was time for closing statements. The prosecution always goes first, whether the trial takes place in a state or, as here, federal court.

"A man may not have intelligence enough to be made responsible, even for a lesser crime; but it is hard, it is very hard to conceive of the individual with any degree of intelligence at all, incapable of comprehending that the head of a great constitutional republic is not to be shot down like a dog," Porter the prosecutor concluded.

The defense attorney took his turn. "Such is the indescribable egotism of this man that he put himself on the same plane as the Savior of mankind and the prophets. There you have the explanation of his applying for the mission at Paris. For this man, in his indescribable egotism, seems to have thought all along that there was nothing in the world too high for him," the defense closed, in arguing for Guiteau to be found insane and not responsible for his actions.

Judge Cox then charged the jury.

This indictment charges the defendant with having murdered James A. Garfield. It becomes my duty to explain to you the nature of the crime charged. Murder is committed where a person of sound memory and discretion unlawfully kills with malice aforethought. Of course, it must be proved first that the death was caused by the act of the accused. It must be further shown that it was caused with malice aforethought.

But this does not mean that the government must prove any special ill will, hatred or grudge on the part of the prisoner towards the deceased. Whenever a homicide is shown to have been committed without lawful authority and with deliberate intent, it is sufficiently proved to have been with malice aforethought.

James Garfield was a homicide victim like anyone else. If the prosecution could show that the defendant committed murder with malice aforethought and was cognizant of his actions, he was liable for a first-degree murder conviction, punishable by death, which no one mentioned, though everyone acknowledged that a death sentence was on the table with a first-degree murder conviction.

Judge Cox continued with his instructions, emphasizing to the jury that while it was the responsibility of the prosecution to prove the guilt of the defendant beyond a reasonable doubt, it was up to the defense to prove insanity.

In the next place, I instruct you that every defendant is presumed innocent until the accusation against him is established by proof. Notwithstanding this presumption of innocence, it is equally true that a defendant is presumed to be sane and have been so at the time when the crime charged against him was committed; that is to say, the government is not bound, as a part of its proofs, to show affirmatively, that the defendant was insane.

As insanity is the exception and most men are sane, the law presumes the latter condition of everybody until some reason is shown to believe the contrary. The burden is therefore on the defendant who sets up an excuse for crime to bring forward his proof, in the first instance, to show that that presumption is a mistake as far as it relates to him.

The crime then, involves three elements—the killing, malice, and a responsible mind in the murderer.

When he had finished, Scoville rose.

"Is it not proper that Your Honor should instruct the jury as to the form of their verdict, if they find him not guilty by reason of insanity?"

Cox turned to the jury.

"If you should think that the prisoner is not guilty by reason of insanity, it is proper for you to say so," Cox instructed the twelve men.

Cox then sent the jury out to consider their verdict on history.[6]

27

"I Am Not Guilty of the Charge
Set Forth in the Indictment"

The jury retired at 4:35 p.m. The testimony had taken two months, with many witnesses. The testimony had primarily reckoned with the results of the bullet from the Bulldog pistol in Guiteau's hand. The jury took an hour to discuss this complex testimony before they reached their verdict. Accompanied by federal marshals and bailiffs, they returned to the jury box at 5:40 p.m.

"Gentlemen of the jury, have you agreed upon a verdict?" the court clerk asked.

"We have," said the foreman, without rising.

"What say you? Is the defendant guilty or not guilty?"

"Guilty as indicted, sir."

People in the gallery applauded the verdict.

"Silence!" cried the bailiffs.

Scoville was on his feet.

"If the court please, if the court please, I desire to have the jury polled."

"Let the jury be polled," Judge Cox ordered.

Each of the jurors was then asked if the defendant was "guilty" or "not guilty." As the last juror's "guilty" rang out in the silent courtroom, so did Guiteau's harsh voice.

"My blood be on the head of that jury; don't you forget it. That is my answer!" he yelled.

Both the judge and the lawyers ignored Guiteau's outburst. He had made similar outbursts throughout the trial. They had gotten to the point where they just ignored him.

"I understand I have the time to file a motion [for a new trial]?" Scoville continued.

"You have four days within which to file the motion," the judge answered.

"God will avenge this outrage!" Guiteau shouted.[1]

As he was led away in shackles, the judge set sentencing a few weeks hence.[2]

February 3, 1882

Charles Guiteau arose in the courtroom to plead for his life. "I am not guilty of the charge set forth in the indictment. It was God's act, not mine, and God will take care of it, and don't let the American people forget it. The American people will roll in blood if I am hung and my body goes in the ground."

Judge Cox looked down from the bench at the defendant. He had been particularly tolerant of Guiteau's outbursts during the trial. He could have had him gagged, but he didn't. He was calm and measured in answering Guiteau with his sentence.

One cannot doubt that you understood the nature and consequence of your crime or that you had the moral capacity to recognize its iniquity. Your own wretched sophistry, not inspiration, overcame the promptings of conscience. It is my duty to pronounce the sentence of the law, that you be taken to the common jail of the District and be kept in confinement and on Friday the 30th of June 1882, you will be taken to the place prepared for the execution, within the walls of said jail, and there between the hours of 12 p.m. and 2 p.m. you be hanged by the neck until dead. And may God have mercy on your soul.

"And may God have mercy on *your* soul," Guiteau reposted sharply. "I had rather stand where I am than where the jury does, or Your Honor does. I am not afraid to die. I know where I stand on this business. I am here as God's man and don't you forget it. God almighty will curse every man who has had anything to do with this act."[3]

June 30, 1882

A short while before the execution, a squad of soldiers entered the jail rotunda. They were there to prepare Guiteau for meeting his Lord. When they came to attention around him with a loud "bang," Guiteau fell over in a dead faint. The prison doctors quickly reacted with a restorative. Someone found a bottle of cheap brandy and they gave it to Guiteau.

"Guiteau was drunk when he ascended the stairs to the scaffold," said eyewitness J. Walter Mitchell, a reporter for the *Times Herald*. Placed on the scaffold, with the trap door beneath his feet, he was surrounded by men in formal dress for the occasion. Guiteau decided to give them a show.

"I am going to the Lordy," he sang drunkenly, as his hands were bound, then his legs a little above the ankles, and then mid-thigh.[4]

Guiteau's head was put in a long, black mask that looked more like a cowl without eye holes. The hangman put the noose around his neck, adjusted it until he was satisfied, then stepped back to the lever, which he jerked. The trapdoor flew open and Guiteau dropped. His neck broke. It took less than a minute and his brain finally disconnected from his body.

Like anyone hung, Guiteau's bladder and sphincter muscle opened up upon death. A doctor came forward to listen to his heart to make sure he was dead. When he was satisfied that he was, he gave the signal to cut the hanged man down.

July 1882

In the July 16, 1882, issue of the *Medical Record*, Bliss published his second article in less than a year ("Feeding per Rectum: As Illustrated in the Case of the Late President Garfield and Others"), defending and extolling his treatment of the president.

This is the article in which he makes his scientifically false claims that Garfield took nourishment by having stuff pumped up his anus and into his intestines. Including blood.

December 1882

Alexander Graham Bell had stood for and become an American citizen, much to his delight.

Charles Guiteau had had his head removed by the doctors

who did his autopsy. It was somewhere in a Washington lab, as scientists examined his brain, looking for some anomaly that would explain his curious behavior.

D. W. Bliss felt like he had been beheaded too. Betrayed was a better word. He was furious that he had billed Congress top dollar for his care of the president and they were balking at the amount. He told a reporter "that while he could not speak of his associates, he could say distinctly for himself that he should not accept the $6,500 [allowed by the Garfield claim board]."

Bliss insisted "[he] would take what his services were worth, or he would go unpaid." He had told Congress that he was making on average $1,500 per month. When Congress was in session, he made up to $3,000 per month. Not only had he solely treated the president for over two months, he had had to suspend his practice to do it, losing in the process six months of earnings.

The board's action was an "insult" to him, a "fraud," in trying to deny him the money he was due. Congress stuck to its guns. Bliss eventually took what the government offered. He continued to practice medicine up until his death in 1889. He was sixty-four years old, and people felt sorry for him.

"The death of Dr. Bliss," wrote the *Democrat*,

> recalls the popular superstition that fate seems to pursue everybody who was even remotely connected with the death of Garfield and the trial and hanging of Guiteau. Dr. Bliss ten years ago was a vigorous, hearty, prosperous man. Since the great patient of his time and skill died, he has suffered nothing but misfortune.
>
> He lost his practice. Congress refused him his fee and gave him but a small one; his wife died; he himself met with a severe array of misfortunes and now he dies suddenly himself. He always thought Congress had treated him shamefully in cutting down his fee and his heirs may get some of the money which is still available and unexpended.[5]

But the story wasn't over yet. In two decades, yet a third president's life and death, would be affected by Bliss's actions.

Over the Rainbow City

Robert Lincoln did not have anything to do with President McKinley's treatment. Instead, after McKinley was shot, he was left alone with his thoughts of his father and James Garfield. Not so John D. Wells.

The President was led to a chair a dozen steps away, and into this he sank, exhausted. His collar and necktie were quickly loosed and his shirt opened at the front. I was considerably excited, inasmuch as the shooting appealed to me, to use what may seem to be a heartless expression, in a business way. I was a newspaper man, and there for the sole purpose of covering the story.

I might look at it from a sentimental viewpoint later. I did not know which to follow, the President or the assassin. Then I concluded to follow the President. I walked to his side, and, seeing the others using their hats in lieu of fans, did the same with mine.

Secretary George Cortelyou was bending over the president. "Cortelyou, you be careful. Tell Mrs. McKinley gently," said the president.

Wells then ran across the room to see what was happening with Czolgosz.

He was "prostrate on the floor. A dozen or more men, detectives and guards, were standing over him, striking and kicking him."

The way Czolgosz was being beaten, he might not even survive to his trial. Wells turned and went back to McKinley's side. McKinley happened to be sitting near where Czolgosz was being severely bludgeoned by the president's men.

"See that no one hurts him," McKinley ordered.

William McKinley was an attorney, another Ohio boy who was a fair man, and he had served with James Garfield in Congress. He was also a smart guy. An ambulance having been summoned, it arrived and took him to a private home to be nursed.

Five years earlier, Wilhelm Roentgen had shown how an X-ray could be used in medical care. Like the induction balance, it was a way to locate a bullet without painful exploration of the body. In fact, there was an X-ray machine at the Pan-American Exposition.

McKinley requested an X-ray to find the bullet, but the president's doctors didn't want to take the chance of moving him back to the exposition. The only portable machine on the planet capable of detecting the bullet was the induction balance.

But it had been discredited. D. W. Bliss had helped see to that. It would eventually be an exhibit in the Smithsonian Institution. And so the doctors operated on President McKinley without knowing where the bullet was.

Eight days after he was shot, William McKinley died from gangrene.[1] He was buried with the death bullet still inside him; his surgeons never located it. The day McKinley died, Alexander Graham Bell wrote about the day in his journal.

1901, Sept. 14, Saturday At B.B. Lab

The sad news was received this morning of the death of President Wm. McKinley. Our flags are at half mast, and draped with black.

He next wrote about the flying experiments he was then conducting.

Our triangular kites in which each cell represents an equilateral triangle, seemed to be indifferent as to their position in the air. We have flown them by strings attached to one corner—we have made one corner heavier than the other by having a double rod, or keel, so as to keep one corner down—but, upon thinking the matter over I fail to see the advantage gained by making these kites fly with one corner down, forming a keel, and the flat aeroplane surface above.

I think one reason why it has seemed most proper to have the kites fly in this way, is the analogy of a ship with its deck above, and its keel below the water. The analogy, however, is probably false, and I am inclined to think that many advantages are to be gained from making our ship fly upside down—deck down, keel up.

The day McKinley died, Bell had been off flying a kite.

It didn't miss Robert Lincoln's attention that he had now been at the sides of three presidents, including his father, after they had been shot. Being that he was Lincoln's only surviving son and a distinguished one at that, he received presidential invitations over the next two decades for various functions. He went, until he changed his mind.

"No, I'm not going, and they'd better not ask me, because there is a certain fatality about presidential functions when I am present."[2]

He finally broke his own rule. In style.

On May 30, 1922, Robert was on the dais at the inauguration of the Lincoln Memorial, in Washington DC, with two presidents in attendance and a vice president who would later become president. President Warren G. Harding was there, as was former president William Howard Taft, then serving as Chief Justice of the Supreme Court. Vice President Calvin Coolidge, who would later become chief executive, was on hand as well.

That day, Alexander Graham Bell was seventy-five years old. He had been in failing health for "several months," the *New York Times* later observed in their obituary, when he died several months later, on August 2, 1922. Perhaps that explains why he was not at the event.

Mabel was so in love with her husband that upon his death, her health failed. Mabel was sixty-five when she died six months later. Though the death certificate didn't say it, she really did die of a broken heart.

This house was on the market in Southern California.

Location: 1001 Buena Vista Street, South Pasadena, 91030
Price: $2.995 million
Year built: 1904
Architects: Greene and Greene
House size: 4,426 square feet, five bedrooms, five bathrooms

It was Lucretia Garfield's house. She had lived there from 1904 until her death on March 14, 1918, when she was eighty-five years old. Her great-great-grandson Hank Garfield wrote the foreword to this book.

James and Lucretia Garfield would have been proud.

ACKNOWLEDGMENTS

Alexander Graham Bell learned one important lesson from the way Western Union tried to rip him off: he made sure constantly to document all his experiments. That is why we have his papers and correspondence regarding the induction balance, and, even more, his comments about Garfield's autopsy. I am equally indebted to Dr. Charles Leale. His first-hand account of treating Lincoln offers eyewitness evidence of the way in which Bliss had been left out of the president's treatment. But Bliss did win out—every historical source says he was one of Lincoln's doctors, implying that he had cared for him, the same as had Leale and the others.

What happened to James Garfield inevitably affected his descendants, including Hank Garfield. Hank has for many years supported my efforts to bring justice to his great-great-grandfather. Because he is a Red Sox fan, he knew how to show patience.

Judy Coppage, a personal friend of Mike Longstreet's, believed that I had something to say that needed to be said. She brought it to Sam Dorrance at Potomac Books, an imprint of the University of Nebraska Press. Tom Swanson and Joeth Zucco steered the ship. Dr. Karen Brown did the bang-up editing job. Emily Wendell kept me honest.

Gerald Posner told me, "Fred, take them off their pedestal." That advice went very, very far.

Michelle and Ray Pollard kept me on track; a Jedi knight kept me sane; and Sara, as always, kept me on my toes.

APPENDIX

The Garfield Agreement of 1872

The complete text of the agreement and further information about the Salish people and the Jocko Reservation can be found at the website for the St. Mary's Mission and Museum (in Stevensville MT) at www.saintmarysmission.org.

AGREEMENT DRAWN UP BY
JAMES A. GARFIELD,
SPECIAL COMMISSIONER
FLATHEAD INDIAN AGENCY, JOCKO RESERVATION
AUGUST 27, 1872

Articles of Agreement made this twenty-seventh day of August, A.D., One thousand, Eight Hundred and Seventy Two between James G. [*sic*] Garfield, Special Commissioner, authorized by the Secretary of the Interior, to carry into execution the provisions of the Act approved June 5th, 1872 for the removal of the Flathead and other Indians from the Bitter Root valley, of the first part, and Charlo, first Chief, and Arlee, second Chief, and Adolphe, third Chief, of the Flatheads, of the second part.

Witnesseth:

Whereas it was provided in the 11th Article of the Treaty concluded at Hell Gate, July 16, 1855, and ratified by the Senate, March 8th, 1859, between the United States and the Flathead, Kootenai and Pend d'Oreille Indians, that the President should cause the Bitter Root Valley above the Lolo Fork to be surveyed and examined, and if in his judgment it should be found better adapted to the wants of the Flathead tribe as a reservation for said tribe, it should be set apart and reserved—and

Whereas the President did on the 11th day of November,

1871, sign his order setting forth that the Bitter Root Valley had been carefully surveyed and examined in accordance with said treaty, and did declare the "it is therefore ordered that all Indians residing in said Bitter Root Valley be removed as soon as practicable to the Jocko Reservation, and that a just compensation be made for improvements made by them in the Bitter Root Valley, and

Whereas, the act of Congress above recited, approved June 5th, 1872 makes provision for such compensation. Therefore it is hereby agreed and covented by the parties to this instrument:

First—That the party of the first part shall cause to be erected Sixty good and substantial houses, twelve feet by sixteen each (if so large a number shall be needed for the accommodation of the tribe). Three of the said houses, viz: for the first, second and third chiefs of said tribe, to be double the size mentioned above. Said houses to be placed on such portion of the Jocko Reservation not already occupied by other Indians, as said Chiefs may select.

Second—that the Superintendent of Indian Affairs for Montana Territory shall cause to be delivered to said Indians six hundred (600) bushels of wheat, the same to be ground, without cost to said Indians into flour, and delivered to them during the first year after their removal, together with such potatoes and other vegetables as can be spared from the Agency farm.

Third—that said Superintendent shall, as soon as practicable, cause suitable portions of land to be enclosed and broken up for said Indians, and shall furnish them with sufficient number of agricultural implements for the cultivation of their grounds.

Fourth—that in carrying out the foregoing agreement, as much as possible shall be done at the Agency by the employees of the government, and none of such labor, or materials or provisions furnished from the Agency shall be charged as money.

Fifth—the whole of the Five Thousand Dollars, in money, now in the hands of the said Superintendent, apportioned for the removal of said Indians, shall be paid to them in such form as their Chiefs shall determine, except such portion as is necessary expended in carrying out the preceding portions of this agreement.

Sixth—that there shall be paid to said tribe of Flathead Indians, the further sum of Fifty Thousand Dollars, as provided in the second section of the act above recited, to be paid in ten annual installments in such manner and material as the President may direct—and no part of the payments herein promised shall in any way affect or modify the full right of said Indians to the payments and annuities now and hereafter due them under existing Treaties.

Seventh—It is understood and agreed that this contract shall in no way interfere with the rights of any member of the Flathead Tribe to take land in the Bitter Root Valley, under the 3 Section of the act above recited.

Eighth—And the party of the second part, hereby agree, that when the houses have been built, as provided in the first clause of this agreement, they will remove the Flathead tribe to said houses (except such as shall take land in the Bitter Root Valley in accordance with the 3rd Section of the act above recited) and will thereafter occupy the Jocko Reservation as their permanent home.

But nothing in this agreement shall deprive said Indians of their full right to hunt and fish in any Indian country where they are now entitled to hunt and fish under existing treaties. Nor shall anything in this agreement be so construed, as to deprive any of said Indians, so removing to the Jocko Reservation, from selling all their improvements in the Bitter Root Valley.

James A. Garfield
Special Com. for the
Removal of the Flatheads
from the Bitter Root Valley

NOTES

Prologue

1. George Alfred Townsend, "President Garfield and his Cabinet," *Frank Leslie's Popular Monthly* 11, no. 5 (May 1881): 4–6.
2. "Robert Todd Lincoln Biography," McDonald's Corporation, access date October 2, 2015, http://www.biography.com/people/robert-todd-lincoln-20989843.
3. "The Buildings," Buffalo History Works, updated December 14, 1998, http://www.eyewitnesstohistory.com/mckinley.htm.
4. "The Assassination of President William McKinley, 1901," John D. Wells, access date 2010, http://www.eyewitnesstohistory.com/mckinley.htm.

1. "Circumstances Have Led Me"

1. Ridpath, *James Garfield*, 21–44.
2. "James A. Garfield," History Channel, http://www.history.com/topics/us-presidents/james-a-garfield.
3. "Doctor Willard Bliss," Men of the 3rd Michigan Infantry, October 24, 2007, http://thirdmichigan.blogspot.com/2007/10/d-willard-bliss.html.
4. "First Lady Biography: Lucretia Garfield," http://www.firstladies.org/biographies/firstladies.aspx?biography=21.
5. Ridpath, *James Garfield*, 82.

2. "First Fruit"

1. During his lifetime, people that knew Alexander Graham Bell referred to him in writing as both "Alec" and "Aleck." For the purposes of clarity and consistency in this book, when the familiar is used, it is Alec.
2. Bruce, *Alexander Graham Bell*, 24.
3. Grosvenor and Wesson, *Alexander Graham Bell*, 15–17.
4. Grosvenor and Wesson, *Alexander Graham Bell*, 17.
5. Grosvenor and Wesson, *Alexander Graham Bell*, 23.

3. "I Am Greatly Perplexed"

1. Ridpath, *James Garfield*, 79–82.
2. James Buchanan's obituary, *New York Times*, June 2, 1869, 5.
3. See Johnny Horton's "The Battle of Bull Run" (1956–60).
4. Phone interview by author with Kevin Sullivan, July 4, 2015.

4. "The Men of the Third Infantry"

1. Sullivan, *Custer's Road to Disaster*, 35.
2. Steve Soper, "Zenas E. Bliss," *Men of the 3rd Michigan Infantry* (blog), October 26, 2007, thirdmichigan.blogspot.com/2007/10/zenas-e-bliss.html.
3. "The First Battle of Bull Run, 1861," Eyewitness to History.com, 2004.
4. Kidd, *Personal Recollections*, 83.
5. Ridpath, *James Garfield*, 91.

5. "To Lose Kentucky"

1. Abraham Lincoln, letter to D. H. Browning, September 22, 1861 in "To Lose Kentucky is to Lose the Whole Game," http://teachingamericanhistory.org/library/document/to-lose-kentucky-is-to-lose-the-whole-game/.
2. "Doctor Willard Bliss," Men of the 3rd Michigan Infantry, October 24, 2007, http://thirdmichigan.blogspot.com/2007/10/d-willard-bliss.html.
3. Ridpath, *James Garfield*, 92–94.

6. "Should Not Have Kept Attacking"

1. Thayer, *From Log Cabin to White House*, 465.
2. Ridpath, *James Garfield*, 118.
3. "Doctor Willard Bliss," Men of the 3rd Michigan Infantry, October 24, 2007, http://thirdmichigan.blogspot.com/2007/10/d-willard-bliss.html.

7. "Why Don't You Plant Flower Seeds?"

1. "Doctor Willard Bliss," Men of the 3rd Michigan Infantry, October 24, 2007, http://thirdmichigan.blogspot.com/2007/10/d-willard-bliss.html.
2. Tarbell, *Life of Abraham Lincoln*, 159.
3. Whitman, *Complete Prose Works*, 30.
4. "Reading 2: Walt Whitman and President Lincoln," National Park Service, accessed July 4, 2015, http://www.nps.gov/nr/twhp/wwwlps/lessons/138lincoln_cottage/138facts2.htm.
5. Tarbell, *Life of Abraham Lincoln*, 159.
6. "Julius P. Garesche," accessed January 3, 2011, http://www.patheos.com/blogs/mcnamarasblog/2011/0"this-faithful-and-devout-catholic-soldier"-lieutenant-colonel-julius-p-garesche-1821-1862.html.
7. "Julius P. Garesche," Civil War Trust, accessed August 2, 2015, http://www.civilwar.org/education/history/biographies/Julius-P-Garesch%c3%a9.html.
8. Fitch, *Annals of the Army of the Cumberland*, 248.
9. "Doctor Willard Bliss," Men of the 3rd Michigan Infantry, October 24, 2007, http://thirdmichigan.blogspot.com/2007/10/d-willard-bliss.html.
10. Walt Whitman, letter to his brother, May 27, 1863 in the Walt Whitman Archive, access date August 3, 2015, whitmanarchive.org.

8. "It Will Indeed Be a Day of Blood"

1. "Letters from Washington," *Sacramento Daily Union* 26, no. 4003 (January 20, 1864).

2. "Doctor Willard Bliss," Men of the 3rd Michigan Infantry, October 24, 2007, http://thirdmichigan.blogspot.com/2007/10/d-willard-bliss.html.

3. Morris, *Better Angel*, 163.

4. "Letters from Washington," *Sacramento Daily Union* 26, no. 4003 (January 20, 1864).

5. "Visitors From Congress," access date August 5, 2015, http://www.mrlincolnswhitehouse.org/www_redesign/inside.asp?id=697&subject ID=2.

6. "Braxton Bragg," Civil War Trust, access date August 5, 2015, http://www.civilwar.org/education/history/biographies/braxton-bragg.html.

7. "Battle of Chickamauga," New Georgia Encyclopedia, last modified October 12, 2015, http://www.georgiaencyclopedia.org/articles/history-archaeology/battle-chickamauga.

8. Ridpath, *James Garfield*, 142–54.

9. "The Republican Majority Is Very Small"

1. Ridpath, *James Garfield*, 154–67.

2. "Abraham Lincoln," Civil War Trust, http://www.civilwar.org/education/history/biographies/abraham-lincoln.html.

3. Ridpath, *James Garfield*, 165 and 166.

4. J. David Hacker, "Decennial Life Tables for the White Population of the United States," U.S. National Library of Medicine, April 1, 2011, http://www.ncbi.nlm.nih.gov/pmc/articles/PMC2885717/?report=reader.

5. "Family: Robert Lincoln," Mr. Lincoln's White House, http://www.mrlincolnswhitehouse.org/inside.asp?ID=16&subjectID=2.

6. "Edwin Booth," HistoryNet, http://www.historynet.com/edwin-booth.

10. "Hands Up!"

1. "Serious Illness of Senator Hicks," *New York Times*, Saturday, February 11, 1865.

2. John DeFerrari, "The Metropolitan," Streets of Washington, December 10, 2009, http://www.streetsofwashington.com/2009/12/metropolitan-aka-browns-marble-hotel.html.

3. "Serious Illness of Senator Hicks," *New York Times*, Saturday, February 11, 1865.

4. Zwicker, *New Hampshire Book of the Dead*, 1741.

5. Papaioannou and Stowell, "Dr. Charles A. Leale's Report on the Assassination of Abraham Lincoln."

6. "Grant and Lee," Civil War Trust, accessed August 6, 2015, http://www.civilwar.org/battlefields/appomattox-courthouse/appomattox-court-house-history/surrender.html.

7. "The Battles of Appomattox Station and Courthouse," Civil War Trust, accessed August 6, 2015, http://www.civilwar.org/battlefields/appomattox-station/appomattox-station-history/the-battles-of-appomattox.html.

8. "Grant and Lee," Civil War Trust, August 7, 2015, http://www.civilwar

.org/battlefields/appomattox-courthouse/appomattox-court-house-history
/surrender.html.

    9. "Surrender at Appomattox, 1865," Ibis Communications, accessed August
7, 2015, http://www.eyewitnesstohistory.com/appomatx.htm.

    10. Roger Norton, Abraham Lincoln's Assassination, December 29, 1996,
http://rogerjnorton.com/Lincoln45.html.

    11. Eaton and Rizio, *Color of Lincoln*, 110.

    12. Papaioannou and Stowell, "Dr. Charles Leale's Report on the Assassi-
nation of Abraham Lincoln."

11. "God Reigns, Washington Still Lives!"

    1. Paige Williams, Special Report: The Assassination of Abraham Lincoln,
"The Closest Source We Have to Really Knowing John Wilkes Booth Is His
Sister," *Smithsonian Magazine*, March 2015.

    2. "What were the prices of tickets at the theater when Lincoln was assas-
sinated?" http://www.nps.gov/foth/faqs.htm.

    3. "The Gun that Murdered Lincoln," from the classic television series star-
ring Jock Mahoney, 1958–59, produced by Desilu, broadcast on CBS, Yancy
Derringer, episode 24, written and directed by Richard Sale.

    4. Claudia Swain, "Little Known Victims of the Lincoln Assassination,"
Boundary Stones, February 22, 2013, http://blogs.weta.org/boundarystones
/2013/02/22/little-known-victims-lincoln-assassination.

    5. Sandberg, *Abraham Lincoln*, 711.

    6. Joshua Zeitz, Special Report: The Assassination of Abraham Lincoln,
"The History of How We Came to Revere Abraham Lincoln," *Smithsonian Magazine*, February 2014, http://www.smithsonianmag.com/history
/history-how-we-came-to-revere-abraham-lincoln-180949447/.

    7. R. C. Drum, Adjutant General, "Joseph K. Barnes," *National Republi-
can*, April 6, 1883.

    8. Papaioannou and Stowell, "Dr. Charles Leale's Report on the Assassi-
nation of Abraham Lincoln."

    9. "Abraham Lincoln Deathbed," Abraham Lincoln Online, 2015, http://
www.abrahamlincolnonline.org/lincoln/education/abed.htm.

    10. James Garfield, *James Garfield Eulogizes Abraham Lincoln*, RAAB
Collection, accessed on August 17, 2015, http://www.raabcollection.com
/abraham-lincoln-autograph/abraham-lincoln-signed-james-garfield-eulo
gizes-abraham-lincoln-second#sthash.MY2scrpC.dpuf.

12. "Going into the Backwoods"

    1. "Visit the Cemetery," at the Highgate Cemetery website, June 4, 2015,
http://highgatecemetery.org/.

    2. Grosvenor and Wesson, *Alexander Graham Bell*, 29–35.

13. "The Doctor Declares"

    1. "Cundurango: The Latest Report from Dr. Bliss," *New York Times*, July 18, 1871.

2. *Grand Rapids Eagle*, October 6, 1871.

3. *Grand Rapids Eagle*, October 6, 1871.

4. "Doctor Willard Bliss," Men of the 3rd Michigan Infantry, October 24, 2007, http://thirdmichigan.blogspot.com/2007/10/d-willard-bliss.html.

5. "Cundurango: The Latest Report from Dr. Bliss," *New York Times*, July 18, 1871.

14. "Be Always Sure You Are Right"

1. "What Happened to Davy Crockett's Rifle?" Guns of the Old West, July 1, 2015, http://www.truewestmagazine.com/2015/07/old-betsy-davy crockett's-first-rifle/.

2. "Remarks of the Honorable David Crockett," CapitolWords, January 24, 2012, http://capitolwords.org/date/2012/01/24/e63-3_remarks-of -the-honorable-david-crockett/.

3. *Annual Report of the Commissioner of Indian Affairs*, Washington: Government Printing Office, 1868, 214.

4. Connell, *Son of the Morning Star*, 187.

5. James Garfield, entry in personal diary, edited by Oliver W. Holmes, in the Library of Congress, Washington DC, 1872.

6. Http://www.kansashistory.us/fordco/batmasterson.html.

7. James Garfield, *Annual Reports of the Department of the Interior*, 1872.

8. James Garfield, personal diary, 1872.

15. "We Should Not Speak of Love"

1. Boston Fire Historical Society, "Great Boston Fire of 1872," https://www .bostonfirehistory.org/firestorygreatfireof1872.html.

2. Letter from Alexander Graham Bell to Alexander Melville Bell, November 19, 1872, Library of Congress, Bell Collection.

3. Grosvenor and Wesson, *Alexander Graham Bell*.

4. Grosvenor and Wesson, *Alexander Graham Bell*.

5. Grosvenor and Wesson, *Alexander Graham Bell*, 40–47.

6. Grosvenor and Wesson, *Alexander Graham Bell*, 52–53.

7. Grosvenor and Wesson, *Alexander Graham Bell*, 56.

8. "A National Geographic Love Story," National Geographic: Voices, February 14, 2012, http://voices.nationalgeographic.com/2012/02/14/an -ng-kind-of-love/.

9. Grosvenor and Wesson, *Alexander Graham Bell*, 56.

10. "Dom Pedro II and America," Library of Congress, Global Gateway, accessed August 20, 2015. http://international.loc.gov/intldl/brhtml/br-1 /br-1-5-2.html.

11. Letter from Mabel Hubbard to Alexander Graham Bell, August 30, 1875, Library of Congress, Bell Collection.

16. "Aye, There's the Rub"

1. "James A. Garfield and the Centennial Exhibition of 1876," the *Garfield*

Observer, August 29, 2014, https://garfieldnps.wordpress.com/2014/08/21/james-a-garfield-and-the-centennial-exposition-of-1876-part-i/.

2. Grosvenor and Wesson, *Alexander Graham Bell*, 65–73.

3. Grosvenor and Wesson, *Alexander Graham Bell*, 88.

4. Grosvenor and Wesson, *Alexander Graham Bell*, 101.

5. "Doctor Willard Bliss," Men of the 3rd Michigan Infantry, October 24, 2007, http://thirdmichigan.blogspot.com/2007/10/d-willard-bliss.html.

17. "Mr. President, Are You Badly Hurt?"

1. Ridpath, *James Garfield*, 507.

2. "John Humphrey Noyes," accessed December 9, 2014, http://www.britannica.com/biography/John-Humphrey-Noyes.

3. "John Singleton Mosby," Civil War Trust, accessed August 29, 2015, http://www.civilwar.org/education/history/biographies/john-singleton-mosby.html.

4. *The Successful American*, vol. 3, part 1 through vol. 4, part 1, January 1, 1900, p. 523.

18. "Intense Excitement and Painful Suspense"

1. Ridpath, *James Garfield*, 540.

2. Bundy, *Life of General James A. Garfield*, 235.

3. R. C. Drum, National Republican, April 6, 1883, http://localhistory.morrisville.edu/sites/gar_post/BarnesJoseph.html.

4. J. S. Billings, Memoir of Joseph Javier Woodward, April 22, 1885, National Academy of Sciences Online, http://www.nasonline.org/publications/biographical-memoirs/memoir-pdfs/woodward-joseph-j.pdf.

5. Ridpath, *James Garfield*, 519–20.

6. *Charlotte Observer*, July 3, 1881.

7. Ridpath, *James Garfield*, 520–23.

8. Description in the Notes of Bell's lecture, "Upon the Electrical Experiments to Determine the Location of the Bullet in the Body of the Late President Garfield," *Telegraphic Journal and Electrical Review* 11, no. 254 (October 7, 1882): 282–83.

9. Ridpath, *James Garfield*, 527–28.

19. Science Should Be Able to Discover"

1. Pendel, *Thirty-Six Years in the White House*, 116, 117.

2. William E. Carter and Merri Sue Carter, February 2009, "Simon Newcomb, America's First Great Astronomer," http://web.calstatela.edu/faculty/kaniol/a360/simon_newcomb_phys_today_Feb2009.pdf.

3. Description in the Notes of Bell's lecture, "Upon the Electrical Experiments to Determine the Location of the Bullet in the Body of the Late President Garfield," *Telegraphic Journal and Electrical Review* 11, no. 254 (October 7, 1882): 282–83.

4. Description in the Notes of Bell's lecture, "Upon the Electrical Experiments to Determine the Location of the Bullet in the Body of the Late Presi-

dent Garfield," *Telegraphic Journal and Electrical Review* 11, no. 254 (October 7, 1882): 282–83.

5. "James A. Garfield: Life in Brief," http://millercenter.org/president/biography/garfield-life-in-brief.

6. Alexander Graham Bell to Mabel Bell, Telegram, July 17, 1881, Library of Congress, Bell Collection.

20. "Papa Has Gone"

1. Letter from Mabel Hubbard Bell to Alexander Graham Bell, July 16, 1881, Library of Congress, Bell Collection.

2. Letter from Alexander Graham Bell to Mabel Hubbard Bell, July 17, 1881, Library of Congress, Bell Collection.

3. Rosen, *Historical Atlas of American Crime*, 133.

4. Letter from Alexander Graham Bell to Mabel Hubbard Bell, July 26, 1881, Library of Congress, Bell Collection.

5. Letter from Mabel Hubbard Bell to Alexander Graham Bell, July 25, 1881, Library of Congress, Bell Collection.

6. Grosvenor and Wesson, *Alexander Graham Bell*, 107.

7. Grosvenor and Wesson, *Alexander Graham Bell*, 107.

21. "She Excites in Me"

1. Letter from Alexander Graham Bell to Mabel Hubbard Bell, July 26, 1881, Library of Congress, Bell Collection.

2. Letter from James Garfield to Eliza Ballou Garfield, August 11, 1881, Library of Congress, Bell Collection.

3. David Leon Hardt, "Life Expectancy Data," September 27, 2006, http://www.nytimes.com/2006/09/27/business/27leonhardt_sidebar.html.

4. "First Lady Biography: Lucretia Garfield," accessed September 3, 2015, http://www.firstladies.org/biographies/firstladies.aspx?biography=21.

5. Noonan, *Bribes*.

22. "Feeding per Rectum"

1. Letter from Mabel Hubbard Bell to Alexander Graham Bell, July 29, 1881, Library of Congress, Bell Collection.

2. Letter from Mabel Hubbard Bell to Alexander Graham Bell, August 1, 1881, Library of Congress, Bell Collection.

3. Rosen, *Historical Atlas of American Crime*, 134.

4. Grosvenor and Wesson, *Alexander Graham Bell*, 107.

5. Bliss, *Feeding per Rectum*.

6. Charles Stewart Roberts, "William Beaumont the Man and the Opportunity," National Center for Biotechnology Information, 1990, http://www.ncbi.nlm.nih.gov/books/NBK459/.

23. "We Were Enabled"

1. Bliss, *Feeding per Rectum*.

2. "A Great Case Reviewed: Dr. Bliss on the Treatment of the Late President," October 6, 1881, http://query.nytimes.com/mem/archive-free/pdf?res=9B05E2D7103CEE3ABC4E53DFB667838A699FDE.

3. Doyle and Swaney, *Lives of James A. Garfield and Chester A. Arthur*, 103.

4. Peskin, *Garfield*, 305.

5. J. David Hacker, "Decennial Life Tables for the White Population of the United States," U.S. National Library of Medicine, April 1, 2011, http://www.ncbi.nlm.nih.gov/pmc/articles/PMC2885717/?report=reader.

6. Grosvenor and Wesson, *Alexander Graham Bell*, 108.

24. "You Are Getting Out of the Woods"

1. Hosterman, *James Abram Garfield*, 309.

2. Ackerman, *Dark Horse*.

3. "The Blog of James A. Garfield," *Garfield Observer*, July 29, 2012, https://garfieldnps.wordpress.com/2012/07/29/long-branch-new-jersey-the-resort-town-that-hosted-president-garfield/.

4. Ridpath, *James Garfield*, 643.

5. Ridpath, *James Garfield*, 655.

6. D. W. Bliss's testimony cited by "The Death of President Garfield," accessed September 9, 2015, http://www.eyewitnesstohistory.com/gar.htm.

25. "Not in Any Part of the Area Explored!"

1. Telegram from Alexander Graham Bell to Mabel Bell, September 19, 1881, Library of Congress, Bell Collection.

2. Pappas and Joharifard, "Did James Garfield Die of Cholecystitis?"

3. "The Death of President Garfield, 1881," EyeWitness to History, access date September 10, 2015, http://www.eyewitnesstohistory.com/gar.htm.

4. Letter from Alexander Graham Bell to Mabel Hubbard Bell, 1881, Library of Congress, Bell Collection.

5. Douglas Lindner, "The Trial of Charles Guiteau," 2007, http://law2.umkc.edu/faculty/projects/ftrials/guiteau/guiteauaccount.html.

6. Alexander, *Life of Charles Guiteau*, 138.

7. Alexander Graham Bell, "Detection of Metallic Masses in the Human Body," *The Electrician*, January 13, 1883.

8. "A Jury of One's Peers," https://www.aclu.org/blog/speakeasy/jury-ones-peers.

26. "I Think the Doctors Did the Work"

1. Hayes et al. *Complete History*, 212.

2. Douglas Lindner, "The Trial of Charles Guiteau," 2007, http://law2.umkc.edu/faculty/projects/ftrials/guiteau/guiteauaccount.html.

3. "Noted Avenger [with apologies to Captain America] Kills Employee," *Los Angeles Herald* 36, no. 11, October 1908, http://cdnc.ucr.edu/cgi-bin/cdnc?a=d&d=LAH19081012.2.7.

4. Cross Examination of Charles Guiteau, excerpts from the trial tran-

script, http://law2.umkc.edu/faculty/projects/ftrials/guiteau/guiteau
transcriptguiteaucrossx.html.

5. D. W. Bliss, "The Story of President Garfield's Illness," *Century Illustrated Monthly*, vol. 1, 1881.

6. Excerpts from the Trial Transcript: Summation of Guiteau, Judge Cox, instructions to the jury, January 25, 1882, http://law2.umkc.edu/faculty /projects/ftrials/guiteau/guiteauaccount.html.

27. "I Am Not Guilty"

1. Excerpts from the Guiteau Trial Transcript: Sentencing, January 25, 1882, http://law2.umkc.edu/faculty/projects/ftrials/guiteau/guiteautranscript sentence.html.

2. H. H. Alexander, *The Trial of Charles Guiteau*, 1882, 844–845.

3. "Excerpts from the Guiteau Trial Transcript: Sentencing," http://law2 .umkc.edu/faculty/projects/ftrials/guiteau/guiteautranscriptsentence.html.

4. Evelyn, Dickson, and Ackerman, *On This Spot*, 28, 29.

5. "Doctor Willard Bliss," Men of the 3rd Michigan Infantry, October 24, 2007, http://thirdmichigan.blogspot.com/2007/10/d-willard-bliss.html.

Epilogue

1. "X-rays at the Exposition," University of Buffalo Libraries, Pan-American Exposition of 1901, accessed September 13, 2015, http://library.buffalo.edu /pan-am/exposition/health/medical/xrays.html.

2. "Famous Helping Hand Was Required to Save Life of Another Lincoln," *Kentucky Civil War Bugle* 8, no. 4 (October–December 2014), http://the kentuckycivilwarbugle.com/2014-4qpages/robertlincoln.html.

BIBLIOGRAPHY

Ackerman, Kenneth D. *Dark Horse: The Surprise Election and Political Murder of President James A. Garfield.* New York: DeCapo Press, 2003.

Alexander, H. H. *The Life of Charles Guiteau and the Official History of the Most Exciting Case on Record.* Philadelphia: National Publishing Company, 1882.

Bell, Alexander Graham. "Upon the Electrical Experiments to Determine the Location of the Bullet in the Body of the late President Garfield; and Upon a Successful Form of Induction Balance for the Painless Detection of Metallic Masses in the Human Body." *American Journal of Science* 25 (1883): 22–61.

Bliss, D. W. *Feeding per Rectum: As Illustrated in the Case of the Late President Garfield.* New York: The Medical Record, 1882.

Bruce, Robert V. *Alexander Graham Bell and the Conquest of Solitude.* New York: Cornell University Press, 1973.

Bundy, Jonas Mills. *The Life of General James A. Garfield.* Louisville KY: Louisville Library Association, 1881.

Connell, Evan S. *Son of the Morning Star: Custer and the Little Bighorn.* New York: North Point Press, 1984.

Doyle, Burton T., and Homer W. Swaney. *Lives of James A. Garfield and Chester A. Arthur.* Washington DC: Rufus A. Darby, 1881.

Eaton, Brian, and Lee Rizio. *Color of Lincoln.* San Jose: Color of Lincoln Publishing, 2008.

Evelyn, Douglas E., Paul Dickson, and S. J. Ackerman. *On This Spot: Pinpointing the Past in Washington.* Washington DC: National Geographic Society, 2008.

Fitch, John. *Annals of the Army of the Cumberland.* Philadelphia: Lippincott, 1864.

Garfield, James A. Papers, 1775–1889. Manuscript Division, Library of Congress, Washington DC.

Grosvenor, Edwin S., and Morgan Wesson. *Alexander Graham Bell: The Life and Times of the Man Who Invented the Telephone.* New York: Harry M. Abrams, 1997.

Hayes, Henry Gillespie. *A Complete History of the Life and Trial of Charles Julius Guiteau, Assassin of President Garfield.* Springfield OH: HardPress, 2012. Reproduction of the 1882 original published by Hubbard Brothers.

Hosterman, Arthur David. *The Life and Times of James Abram Garfield: Twentieth President of the United States*. Springfield OH: Farm and Fireside, 1882.

Kidd, James Harvey. *Personal Recollections of a Cavalryman with Custer's Michigan Cavalry*. Ionia MI: Sentinel Printing, 1908.

Morris, Roy. *The Better Angel: Walt Whitman in the Civil War*. Oxford UK: Oxford University Press, 2000.

Ogilvie, John Stuart. *History of the Attempted Assassination of James A. Garfield*. New York: J. S. Ogilvie, 1881.

Noonan, John Thomas. *Bribes*. Oakland CA: University of California Press, 1987.

Papaioannou, H. I., and D. W. Stowell. "Dr. Charles Leale's Report on the Assassination of Abraham Lincoln." *Journal of the Abraham Lincoln Association* 34, no. 1 (Winter 2013): 40–53.

Pappas, Theodore N., and Shahrzad Joharifard. "Did James Garfield Die of Cholecystitis?" *American Journal of Surgery* 206, no. 4 (2013): 613–18.

Pendel, Thomas F. *Thirty-Six Years in the White House*. Washington DC: Neale Publishing, 1902.

Peskin, Allen. *Garfield*. Kent OH: Kent State University Press, 1998.

Ridpath, John Clark. *The Life and Work of James A. Garfield: Twentieth President of the United States*. Cincinnati: Jones Brothers, 1881.

Rosen, Fred. *The Historical Atlas of American Crime*. New York: Facts on File, 2005.

Sandburg, Carl. *Abraham Lincoln*. New York: Dell, 1963.

Sullivan, Kevin. *Custer's Road to Disaster: The Path to Little Bighorn*. Guilford CT: Globe Pequot, 2013.

Tarbell, Ida. *The Life of Abraham Lincoln*. New York: Lincoln Memorial Association, 1900.

Thayer, William Makepeace. *From Log-Cabin to White House: Life of James A. Garfield*. London and Melbourne: Ward, Lock, and Co., 1920.

Whitman, Walt, *The Complete Prose Works of Walt Whitman*. New York: G. P. Putnam's, 1920.

Zwicker, Roxie. *New Hampshire Book of the Dead: Graveyard Legends and Lore*. Mount Pleasant SC: History Press, 2012.

INDEX

Brown, Joseph Stanley, 134, 138
Buell, Don Carlos, 30–34, 38
buffalo. *See* Pan-American Exposition
Bull Run, 22–27, 31, 39, 42, 44, 55, 69, 120,
    128. *See also* Bliss, Dr.
    Doctor Willard
    (DW); Custer, George Armstrong
Bunn, Annie, 122, 123. *See also* Guiteau,
    Charles
Butler, Nicholas Murray, 18

Centennial Exposition of Philadelphia,
    112–16. *See also* Bell, Alexander Gra-
    ham; Custer, George Armstrong
Chandler, Zachariah, 42
Chickamauga, 52–61, 172. *See also* Gar-
    field, James Abram
Conkling, Roscoe, 123, 153
Coppage, Richard Paul, 34
Cortelyou, George, 193
Cox, Walter, 179–80, 186–89
Crane, Major Charles Henry, 83
Cranor, Jonathan, 34–36
Creek War, 98–99. *See also* Crockett,
    David (Davy); Jackson, Andrew
Crockett, David (Davy), 99, 104
Cundurango, 91–97
Custer, George Armstrong, 22, 23, 25, 69,
    70, 84, 100, 102, 112–14, 117
Czolgosz, Leon, 19, 193

Davis, Jefferson, 29, 30
Dennison, William, 21, 27
Dom Pedro II, 110, 115, 116

Earp, Wyatt Berry Stapp, 73, 101
Elberon NJ, 155, 169–75
Ellis, Alexander, 86
English, Samuel D., 27
explore. *See* induction balance

Flathead tribe, 99, 100, 101–4
Foote, Allen Ripley, 40, 41
Ford, John T., 65, 75
Ford's Theatre, 72, 75–80
Fort Sumter, 19, 20, 22, 29

Garesche, Julius, 46, 47, 51
Garfield, Abram, 3, 4, 12, 52, 105
Garfield, Eliza (née Ballou), 3, 4, 10,
    18, 19
Garfield, Hank, 196
Garfield, James Abram: affair, 15;

attempted assassination, 19, 20, 119–
    25; autopsy, 177; and Alexander Gra-
    ham Bell, xv, xvi, xx, 6, 127–41, 147,
    149–51, 157–61, 169, 170, 173, 174, 176,
    184–85, 190, 194; birth and early life,
    3–6; and D. Willard Bliss, 6, 15, 20, 134–
    38, 141–51, 159, 176–78; Lucia Calhoun,
    152; children, 120; Civil War service,
    27–40, 51–63; death, 171–74; Flathead
    Treaty, 98–104; elected to House of
    Representatives, 50; elected to Ohio
    State Senate, 17, 18; murder, 184–87;
    Centennial Exposition of Philadelphia,
    113; Williams College, 8–10
Garfield, Lucretia "Crete," 8, 9, 17, 20,
    28, 40, 113, 119, 126, 127, 130, 137, 152–
    56, 166, 169–71, 174, 175, 196
Grand Rapids MI, 7, 31, 94, 95, 97, 121
Grant, Orville, 112
Grant, Ulysses S., 19, 39, 61, 65, 68, 69–
    71, 76, 100–102, 115, 120, 124, 170, 171
Gray, Elisha, 108, 114, 116, 167
Guiteau, Charles, 20, 121–25, 154, 155,
    166, 176, 178–91
Guiteau, Frances, 122, 123, 178

Hale, John P., 49, 50, 51, 67, 68, 72
Hale, Lucy, 68, 72
Half-Breeds, 120, 123
Hannibal, 34, 36
Harris, Clara, 76, 77
Hay, John, 82
Hazen, William S., 47
Herdman, Annie, 13
Herdman, Ben, 13–15
Herdman, John, 13–15
Hubbard, Gardiner Greene, 88, 106, 108,
    109, 117, 133
Hicks, Thomas Holliday, 66, 67

Indian Removal Act, 98, 99
induction balance, 138, 144, 148, 149–51,
    157, 158, 159, 167, 177–79, 184, 185, 194

Jackson, Andrew, 98–100, 124
Jackson, Thomas "Stonewall," 23, 24
Jefferson, Thomas, 19
Jones, Bill (the Avenger), 181, 182
Judge Advocate General, 48, 167

Leale, Charles, 50, 68, 72, 76, 77–83,
    127, 197